ABANDONED PLACES

ABANDONED PLACES

Published by Collins
An imprint of HarperCollins Publishers
Westerhill Road
Bishopbriggs
Glasgow G64 2QT
www.harpercollins.co.uk

First edition 2015

A catalogue record for this book
is available from the British Library.

ISBN   978-0-00-813659-8

10 9 8 7 6 5 4 3 2 1

Printed in Hong Kong

If you would like to comment on any
aspect of this book, please contact us
at the above address or online:

email: collinsmaps@harpercollins.co.uk
 facebook.com/collinsmaps
 @collinsmaps

Collins

ABANDONED PLACES

60 STORIES OF PLACES WHERE TIME HAS STOPPED

RICHARD HAPPER

CONTENTS

Places listed chronologically by the approximate
date by which they became abandoned

From Antarctic bays bound by a frozen sea to the most parched deserts on earth, from monsoon-drenched estuaries to wind-whipped Atlantic islands, there are places that humans have settled, thrived in, and then abruptly departed from. These abandoned places lie deep underground, on the highest mountain tops, in the middle of our biggest cities, in our suburbs, on our doorsteps. They are all around us, but most of the time we pass them by. Yet when we take the time to look, to explore, we find new worlds that are endlessly fascinating. What brought people to this place? How did they survive? What was life here *really* like? Perhaps most intriguingly of all – why did they leave?

That question is answered in myriad ways. War. Natural disaster. Economic pressure. Fashion. Political games-manship. Greener grass elsewhere. Human foolishness. Every derelict settlement is an empire in miniature that tells its own story of glorious rise and humble fall. Here we present sixty of those intriguing tales, illustrated with photographs that perfectly capture the haunting echoes of lives long forgotten. If there can be no true beauty without decay, then these abandoned places are, in their way, some of the most beautiful places on earth

PETRA

JORDAN

Petra

DATE ABANDONED	TYPE OF PLACE	LOCATION	REASON	INHABITANTS	CURRENT STATUS
AD 663	City	Jordan	Environmental/ Economic	20,000	UNESCO World Heritage Site

THREE CENTURIES BEFORE CHRIST'S BIRTH, A TRIBE OF NOMADS DECIDED TO CUT THEMSELVES A CITY FROM BARE ROCK. ABANDONED AND LOST FOR A MILLENNIUM, THEIR CAPITAL WAS REDISCOVERED IN THE NINETEENTH CENTURY AND IS NOW RECOGNIZED AS ONE OF THE WORLD'S OUTSTANDING CULTURAL WONDERS.

The rose-red city half as old as time

It is called *Petra* in Greek and *Sela* in Hebrew; both mean 'rock' and few places have as simple and as beautifully apt a name. For this city that once housed 20,000 prosperous souls was carved out of, and into, the red sandstone cliffs of a desert gorge over 2,000 years ago.

Most abandoned places have a short life. It is the very nature of their derelict existence: they have been let go, lost, left to the entropic power of nature. Petra, however, is almost as magnificent now as it was two millennia ago.

It is mentioned twice in the Bible and Arab tradition maintains that Petra is where Moses (Musa) struck his staff on a rock and water came forth. Even then it was a wonder: one of the wealthiest cities in the ancient world flourishing in one of the harshest climates on earth. Today it is a magnificently preserved picture of an ancient civilization and a thrilling reminder that not everything we abandon need be lost.

The wanderers settle down

The Nabataeans were originally nomadic spice traders of the south Levant and north Arabia.

They controlled a loosely structured trade network with oases as hubs linked by caravan routes through the surrounding desert.

Around 300 BC, they decided to develop a more state-like kingdom and swiftly constructed Petra as their capital city. The fortress-like location of towering rocks and narrow gullies certainly made for a wonderful defensive site, but there was one major problem: water.

Water management

It may be surrounded on all sides by dry, searing desert, but Petra owes its existence to water. Or rather, to the skill and ingenuity of the Nabataeans in gathering that most precious of commodities and bringing it to their city. When rain does fall here, it creates flash floods that rip through the landscape, carving its distinctive gullies and gorges. For most people that rain would be too rare and too destructive to be of any use.

The Nabataeans thought differently, and they built an ingenious system of conduits, dams, cisterns and pipes to channel and store the rain and spring water from a wide area. This vast plumbing network turned a meagre 15 cm

The façade of Al Khazneh ('The Treasury') is 40 m (131 ft) high. Its position deep in a gorge has helped protect it from erosion.

(6 inches) of annual precipitation into a constant water supply that could deliver an estimated 12 million gallons of fresh water a day. In effect, they had created an artificial oasis. Its water supported the people of Petra – and was vital to travellers, which helped make the city rich.

Petra was located at the junction of a trade route to Asia and another to Arabia. These were the motorways of their day, along which caravans of 2,500 camels, up to 8 km (5 miles) in length, carried spices, cloth, ivory, metals and incense such as frankincense and myrrh. Petra was an ideal rest and refreshment point for these travellers and, as with any service station, the Nabataeans ensured they profited from their visitors.

By 100 BC the Nabataeans had control of the spice trade and they used their burgeoning wealth to expand their remarkable city. Petra became a metropolis of temples, monuments, altars, houses, and banquet halls carved into the sandstone cliffs. There are 3,000 carved tombs and the open-air theatre could seat 8,000 people.

The rock shakes
Like all empires, the Nabataean dynasty eventually had its fall. Petra was taken within the arms of the Roman Empire in AD 106 and at first flourished in the relation-ship; the city was at the height of its wealth and influence around AD 200. However, the city of Palmyra gradually drew Arabian trade away from Petra, which declined as a trading hub.

In AD 363 there was a cataclysmic earthquake that cracked beautifully carved facades, brought rocks tumbling from walls and fractured the seats in the theatre. Although people continued to live here, the city never fully recovered from this shock.

By the fifth century the Nabataeans had converted from their own faith to Christianity and Petra became a renowned religious settlement within the Byzantine realm. But by AD 663 even the pilgrims had ceased to come and the city was deserted.

The city lives again
The city slept in its desert canyon for nearly a millennium, forgotten by the wider world. It was rediscovered by an adventurous 27-year-old Swiss traveller, Johann Ludwig Burckhardt, in 1812. He spent years learning fluent Arabic and had disguised himself as a Bedouin to explore as far off the beaten track as possible. Tales of the lost city's mystical beauty captured the Victorian imagination, and it was famously described as 'a rose-red city half as old as time' in a poem by John William Burgon.

In the First World War, Petra was at the centre of an Arabian revolt against the Ottoman regime. British Army officer

T. E. Lawrence, better known as Lawrence of Arabia, helped drum up support amongst the Bedouins living in the area to rout the Turkish forces.

Exploring the site

Few cities on earth have as spectacular an entrance as Petra. It is approached through the Siq, a sinuous gorge that snakes for 1.2 km (0.75 miles) between gloomy cliffs up to 182 m (597 ft) high. In some places the Siq (meaning 'the Shaft') is only 3 m (9.8 ft) wide, but this split in the mountain is the main way of accessing the city.

Visitors pad through the sandy darkness to finally emerge in a blinding cathedral of light and come face to face with one of Petra's most famous monuments: Al Khazneh ('The Treasury'). This was not a place of business, but rather a crypt built around the time of Christ. It later got its name from a story about bandits who had hidden gold in one of the urns carved high on the facade. Today this urn is pocked with bullet holes made by Bedouins trying to shatter it and release the treasure. In fact, the urn is solid sandstone. The Treasury's huge pillars and pediment are of Greek influence in their design, like many of the buildings in Petra.

Another spectacular carved building is the monastery (actually a temple), which is cut into a hilltop an hour's climb from the main city. The scale of the stone-carving here is truly awe-inspiring: the monastery's huge facade is 50 m (165 ft) square and its doorway is as tall as most houses.

Cut into Petra's East Cliff are the Royal Tombs, a group of large and impressive facades. In the warm ruby light of late afternoon the whole cliff here seems to shimmer and glow.

The secrets that sleep on

Film lovers will be aware of Petra's starring role in many motion pictures. These appearances, and its regular inclusion in new 'Wonders of the World' lists, have widened its fame and made it one of the best known abandoned places. Today, Petra is the most visited place in Jordan and a UNESCO World Heritage Site.

However, one of the most intriguing things about Petra is how much more of it is yet to be discovered. Only 15 per cent of the city has been explored by archaeologists; the vast majority remains underground and untouched, as it has been since antiquity.

ABOVE LEFT: The Urn Tomb, first of the Royal Tombs, is built high up on the mountain side.

ABOVE: The Treasury by night. Behind the facade is a large square room; Indiana Jones found the Holy Grail inside.

MACHU PICCHU

PERU

Machu Picchu

DATE ABANDONED	TYPE OF PLACE	LOCATION	REASON	INHABITANTS	CURRENT STATUS
Sixteenth century	Inca city	Peru	Disease/Invasion	c. 1,000	UNESCO World Heritage Site

CROWNING A SHEER-SIDED PERUVIAN MOUNTAIN IS MACHU PICCHU, AN EXTRAORDINARY EXPRESSION OF ENGINEERING SKILL AND RELIGIOUS DEVOTION THAT WAS ABANDONED ONLY 100 YEARS AFTER ITS CONSTRUCTION. THE INVADING SPANISH NEVER FOUND THE CITY, BUT THE DESTRUCTION THEY BROUGHT KILLED IT NONETHELESS.

The palace in the peaks

It was a royal Inca estate and religious retreat that just happened to be perched on a precipitous mountain ridge at 2,430 m (7,970 ft) above sea level. Machu Picchu was completed around 1450, and flourished as a self-sustaining stronghold of 1,000 souls for 100 years. Then it was abruptly abandoned during a time of catastrophic population collapse. Today its enigmatic remains are among the most beautiful and spectacular of all lost civilizations.

It's hard to imagine a site with better natural defensive protection. The Urubamba River encircles the site on three sides, at the bottom of cliffs that drop vertically for 450 m (1,480 ft). On the fourth side is a nearly impassable mountain peak.

There was a secret entrance via rope bridge, known only to the Inca army. If an offensive army were to approach they would be seen miles away. When they arrived they would have an unpleasant climb up a near-sheer, heavily vegetated cliff face. Any attempt to starve out the inhabitants would be doomed to failure – the city had enough arable land within its walls to feed its population four times over, and fresh water is not a problem in this misty, rainy area.

The design of the city itself is ingenious. The high hillsides were cut into terraces, to increase the arable land available and to decrease the incidence of landslides. As well as the agricultural zone, Machu Picchu had an urban area. Here were temples, palaces, workshops, storehouses and homes made of expertly dressed stone. Blocks, some weighing up to 50 tonnes, were cut with millimetre-precision to form faultless joints without the use of any mortar. In many places a small gap has been left in the stonework to allow walls to move and flex in an earthquake, thus absorbing much of the destructive force.

Mountain-worship rituals

Religion was part of the everyday fabric of Inca life and Machu Picchu itself was a physical expression of their beliefs. This was a city-shrine to the gods, a clifftop cathedral that stood in symbiosis with the mountain landscape surrounding it. There are several 'replica stones' throughout the city; these have been sculpted to echo the shape of the mountain peaks behind them. They were likely a sign of the Incas' devotion to the mountain god Apo.

The Intiwatana stone was an astronomic clock or calendar with a protruding gnomon that cast a shadow onto a broad

base; the positioning of the shadow marked the June and December solstices. The stone also functioned as an altar.

The end of an ancient empire

When a fleet of Spanish ships reached the Spanish colony in Panama in 1520, on board were diseases unknown in the Americas. Smallpox, measles and other contagions ripped through the native populations.

The Inca Empire was then at its height under the ruler Huayna Capac. It stretched for a thousand miles from north to south (covering much of present-day Bolivia, Peru, Argentina, Chile, Ecuador, and Colombia), and incorporated 200 different ethnic groups.

The Spanish didn't get to Peru until 1532, when Francisco Pizarro landed on the north coast with 260 fellow Spaniards. By that time, however, smallpox, measles and civil war had already killed millions of people – two-thirds of the population of this vast empire perished. The great leader Capac was one of the dead, and his passing divided the Inca Empire; a brutal civil war erupted over which of his sons would rule.

The mighty Inca armies were in disarray and the carefully organized state administration was in tatters. The Spanish started looting the temples and palaces in a virtual gold rush, as well as killing the Inca leaders.

No men for maintenance

Travel routes in the mountainous area around Machu Picchu require constant maintenance to be kept open. The area gets more than 1.8 m (70 inches) of rain a year, which frequently washes away roads and trails. Fast-growing vegetation will block cleared trails in a season. Even the modern roads and railway are regularly breached by rockslides and water damage. With the available manpower slashed by plague and war, maintaining such an exotic settlement as Machu Picchu was simply not a priority to the fractured Inca state.

There was a large rebellion against the controlling Spanish in 1536. As the Spanish fought to quell the uprising, many Inca fled into the remote Peruvian hinterlands. To discourage Spanish pursuit, many tracks and settlements were deliberately destroyed, including those at the start of the now famous Inca Trail that leads to Machu Picchu. The city itself would by now have been overgrown by vegetation and the route in to it blocked by landslides.

No one told the Spanish about its location and they never found it themselves, neither then nor at any point during the colonial period. Machu Picchu would be lost to the outside world for nearly four centuries.

'Indiana' Bingham

'It seemed almost incredible that this city [Machu Picchu], only five days' journey from Cuzco, should have remained so long undescribed and comparatively unknown.'
Hiram Bingham, writing in Harper's Monthly, 1913

The best-known narrative of the rediscovery is a tale that truly fires the imagination. Hiram Bingham III was a mountaineer, explorer and Yale University academic who led an American expedition that planned to outdo the discoveries of famous British travellers such as David Livingstone.

In 1911 he led a group that set out from Cuzco in search of lost Inca cities. Bingham got lucky, receiving a tip-off from a local about some hilltop ruins deep in the jungle. On a humid July afternoon, Bingham traversed plunging rapids on a log bridge, hacked his way up a jungled slope and finally crested a rocky promontory, to suddenly clap eyes on the magnificent remains of Machu Picchu.

He may not have been the first outsider to visit the lost city, but he was the first to fully explore its treasures, and it was he who made it known to the wider world. On a second visit to the site he cleared the ruins of vegetation and photographed the city. Although Bingham also promptly removed cartloads of artefacts, mummies, stone carvings and other precious Inca relics, he was at least an academic and much of the booty ended up at Yale, where it could be studied and preserved. He wrote about his finds in the *National Geographic*, and the world at large was entranced by this lost Inca city in the jungle.

Educated, bold and handsome, it was Bingham who became the real-life model for the fictional bullwhip-cracking adventurer Indiana Jones.

The story in the stones

Machu Picchu is a UNESCO World Heritage Site and a favourite destination of travellers to South America. To most visitors it will never seem at all abandoned. Its story, however, is a sobering one of disease, dereliction and the downfall of one of the world's greatest ever empires.

EASTER ISLAND

Easter Island

CHILE

DATE ABANDONED	TYPE OF PLACE	LOCATION	REASON	INHABITANTS	CURRENT STATUS
1550–1700	Island	Pacific Ocean	Man-made ecological disaster	15,000	UNESCO World Heritage Site

TO THE FIRST VISITORS IT WAS AN EXTRAORDINARY WORLD OF ABANDONMENT. A CIVILIZATION BEYOND THE EDGE OF THE SEA HAD APPARENTLY BEEN CREATED AND THEN HAD CHILLINGLY DECLINED – BUT THE TRUTH OF WHERE ITS PEOPLE WENT IS MORE FRIGHTENING THAN THE MYSTERY.

Moai lined up on their *ahu* – they face inland.

Where did the sculptors go?

'These stone figures caused us to be filled with wonder, for we could not understand how it was possible that people who are destitute of heavy or thick timber, and also of stout cordage, out of which to construct gear, had been able to erect them.'

So wrote the Dutch explorer Jacob Roggeveen on Easter Sunday, 1722. He had just landed on a rather barren isle with no large trees and a population of around 2,000 people. They had few tools and no mechanical devices. They did not know about the wheel. Their canoes were flimsy and so poorly constructed that they had to be constantly baled out just to stay afloat.

Yet Roggeveen was astonished to see that the island was dotted with hundreds of gigantic stone statues. The islanders had worshipped these *moai*, by lighting fires at their bases and prostrating themselves to the rising sun.

There were no trees – so how could the inhabitants have made timber for scaffolding and rollers, or thick ropes for hauling the stones? How could a society that was struggling for food spare the time to make and move these gargantuan statues? They obviously couldn't,

and yet the statues were all upright, clear of vegetation and relatively unweathered. This proved that a great civilization had occupied the island in the very recent past. So where had it gone?

Later explorers found a factory-quarry where the *moai* were cut out of tuff, a compressed volcanic ash. There were dozens of incomplete *moai* half cut from the rock. Stone tools littered the quarry floor. Several completed *moai* stood outside the quarry ready for transport to their destination. Had a creative, determined and accomplished people just upped and vanished?

Easter Island is unique among deserted settlements in that it presented its abandonment as a mystery to be solved.

Brave new world

One of the most remarkable things about Easter Island is that it was ever inhabited in the first place. It is one of the most remote populated islands in the world: the nearest inhabited place is Pitcairn Island 2,075 km (1,289 miles) away, while the closest point on the Chilean mainland is 3,512 km (2,182 miles) away.

The only source of fresh water on the island: a volcanic crater.

Humanity first arrived here by canoe from the Marquesas Islands, 3,200 km (2,000 miles) to the west, in AD 1200. At first, life was good for the Rapa Nui, as the inhabitants were known. Pollen analysis has shown that the island was once thickly wooded, and had at least three tree species that grew up to 15 m (49 ft) high. Palms could be felled for the building of large canoes, and the hauhau tree could be used to make ropes. There was an abundance of nesting seabirds and fish. Sturdy canoes enabled the fishermen to take porpoises, which became a vital part of the islanders' diet.

With ample food for survival the population surged as high as 15,000–20,000. The Rapa Nui had spare time, which they spent making *moai*. This process was not easy and required great organization: the best stone to carve figures from was found at one site; the preferred rock for the headpieces in a different quarry. The tools were made in yet another location.

Images of the dead

The Rapa Nui sculpted 887 *moai*. The completed figures were transported over rough, hilly ground to sites all around the island's coast. There are competing theories about how this was done. The prevailing thinking was that great numbers of trees were felled to create rollers. The *moai* were then placed on skids or sleds and pulled across the rollers. Other studies maintain that they were walked to their destinations using a rocking technique controlled by teams using ropes.

At their destination they were placed on stone platforms and aligned to face the island's interior. They were erected to represent the spirits of ancestors, watching over their descendants.

The tallest *moai* that the islanders erected stood 10 m (33 ft) high and weighed 82 tonnes; but a partially carved sculpture, found abandoned in the quarry, would have stood 21 m (69 ft) high and weighed 270 tonnes.

The island's population was organized into clans, and *moai* creation became an artistic battle for tribal bragging rights: the clan that erected the largest and greatest number of *moai* could claim the highest status.

As *moai* production spiralled into a virtual frenzy, huge numbers of mature trees must have been brought down. Trees were also being used as fuel for fires and being felled to create fields. The consumption of natural resources began to exceed the rate at which those resources could be regrown. Around the year 1500, the shortage of trees meant many people were living in caves rather than huts. A century later the island was almost completely deforested.

There will have been a point when the islanders realized they were in trouble. The island is only 20 km (12 miles) across and its central peak has a commanding view. It would have been easy to see where the remaining groves of trees were. The man who felled the last tree must have known the irreversible step he was taking.

Now no more *moai* could be erected. No more canoes could be built, so there would be no more porpoise to eat and no exodus to a promised land.

The loss of the trees also led to the depletion of nutrients in the soil, which reduced crop yield. Food became scarce. Society could no longer afford the luxury of statue-building and so it stopped. With its resources stripped, the island could not support 15,000 people. The Rapa Nui began to die.

A hard lesson to learn

The mysterious abandonment found by the Europeans was therefore more of a slow suicide — and a sobering example of how devastating a man-made ecological disaster can be. In just 400 years a fertile island paradise had been stripped to a husk.

Unfortunately for the Rapa Nui, life was about to get even worse. Slave raids from Peru, diseases brought by visitors and maltreatment all reduced the population further. By 1877 there were only 111 people on the island.

The island's history since then has been far from straight-forward, but today there are 5,800 inhabitants with descendants of the Rapa Nui accounting for around 60 per cent of the population.

Modern-day visitors make the five hour plane trip out into the Pacific to find a strikingly beautiful island with dramatic cliffs, plunging headlands and rolling swards of grass.

They also marvel at the abandoned *moai*, the physical remains of a ghost culture. The sculptors left testaments to their industry and ingenuity, but precious few explanations for their actions. For the strange irony of the Rapa Nui is that they adapted to live in relative ease so far from other cultures as to be in another world, and yet they couldn't live with themselves.

Will future civilizations wonder where we went?

Moai abandoned before they reached their *ahu* (coastal platforms).

ANI

DATE ABANDONED	TYPE OF PLACE	LOCATION	REASON	INHABITANTS	CURRENT STATUS
Eighteenth century	Medieval city	Turkey	Political	c. 200,000	Ruined

A MILLENNIUM AGO THIS WAS THE CAPITAL CITY OF AN EMPIRE THAT STRETCHED FOR HUNDREDS OF KILOMETRES ACROSS EURASIA. IT SURVIVED VIOLENT CENTURIES OF CLASHING KINGS ONLY TO BE FORGOTTEN WHEN THOSE EMPIRES THEMSELVES FADED. NOW IT LIVES ON IN RUINS, FAR FROM THE TOURIST ATTRACTIONS OF TURKEY, A GILDED SHADOW OF ITS FORMER POWER AND GLORY.

The medieval megacity

There were few more magnificent cities anywhere in the world in AD 1000. Perhaps Baghdad could boast the same architectural majesty, and maybe Constantinople had a similar wealth of international trade. But Rome was in ruins, London was a mere Saxon market town and New York was a wooded island. This is Ani: the key military stronghold, the capital city and the cultural heart of a mighty Armenian empire.

Ani lies deep in eastern Turkey, over 1,450 km (900 miles) from Istanbul. Even the nearest town, Kars, is 48 km (30 miles) away. There is precious little in the hinterland but sheep and goats. The plains here roll on and on in every direction, only ended at last by a horizon of slumbering mountains. This feels a long way from civilization; yet a millennium ago it was the centre of one.

The city of 1001 churches

Just before the Norman kings expanded their rule into England, the Bagratuni royal dynasty was crushing local tribal leaders in the area between the Black Sea, Caspian Sea and eastern

Mediterranean to create an empire of their own. From AD 961 to AD 1045, Ani was the undisputed capital city of a kingdom that stretched for over 800 km (500 miles) from west to east and 600 km (373 miles) from north to south – a territory that would now include Armenia, eastern Turkey and parts of Azerbaijan, Georgia and northern Iran.

The city was blessed with a superb defensive situation: a steep-sided triangular plateau rising from the ravine of the Akhurian River and the Bostanlar Valley. It also happened to lie at a nexus of trade routes that connected Syria and Byzantium with Persia and Central Asia. The canny Bagratuni capitalized on this location to transform the city into a trade hub close to the Silk Road.

When the seat of Armenian Catholicism relocated to Ani in 992, the city also became the centre of a religious golden age. Churches popped up like desert flowers after a flood, and there were no fewer than twelve bishops within the city leading the faithful in prayer. Ani was famous throughout the region as the 'City of 1001 Churches' and the 'City of Forty Gates'.

RIGHT: Earthquakes have shattered the abandoned churches, mosques and walls of Ani.

OVERLEAF: The church of St Gregory of Tigran Honents looks out over the river gorge and the empty plain beyond.

It was also the sacred resting place of the Bagratuni kings, with an extensive royal mausoleum. The city's population grew from around 50,000 in the tenth century to well over 100,000 a hundred years later. It probably topped 200,000 at its peak.

Trophy of the empire builders

The city's strategic location made it a pawn in a vast Eurasian game of chess. It was fought over, sacrificed, taken, even promoted to the status of a queen. The names of the nations fighting changed over the centuries, but Ani saw them all come and go.

From 1044 it came under a wave of Byzantine attacks. In 1064 the town was captured and the inhabitants put to the sword by Seljuk Turks. Over the next 200 years it was owned by Muslim Kurds, Georgians and then Mongols. In the fourteenth century Ani was ruled by another Turkish dynasty, and then the Persians took over, before it became part of the mighty Ottoman Empire in 1579.

By now the city's day in the sun was dimming into its twilight. The earth's great empires now lay elsewhere. By the time the site was completely abandoned in 1750, there was only the equivalent of a small town left within the walls.

Lost and found

Ani slumbered in its little nook for a century or so. It was then rediscovered by delighted archaeologists and excavated in 1893. Several thousand of its most important treasures were uncovered and removed before the site could be looted, as happened in the First World War. At the end of that conflict the city was briefly back in Armenian hands before finally being incorporated into Turkey in 1921.

Today the best-preserved monument in the city is the church of St Gregory of Tigran Honents, completed in 1215. On its outer walls, elaborate animal carvings frame panels filled with ancient text. Inside, its frescos still shine with azure, gold and crimson hues as daylight floods the chamber through windows high in the central tower.

Several other churches stand in various states of preservation. A couple look ready to welcome worshippers; some are cloaked in grasses and lichens. The Church of the Redeemer stands like one half of a huge nutshell, its inside exposed to the elements; the church was cleaved in two by a lightning bolt in the 1950s. The rubble from the fallen half has been heaped forlornly in a poor attempt at protecting the half that remains standing.

The Cathedral of Ani has fared better. This architecturally stunning building was completed in AD 1001 and is famed for its pointed arches and clustered piers. These long predate the gothic style of architecture, which would eventually make such features commonplace.

Just down the street from the cathedral is the mosque of Minuchir, the first mosque to be built on the Anatolian plateau. Its 1,000-year-old minaret survives intact along with much of its prayer hall.

Ani was once encircled by powerful defensive walls, and many of these battlements and towers still stand. The walls were doubled in thickness at the northern side where the city was not protected by a river or ravine. Today these sections remain … ready to face an enemy that will never come.

There are also the remains of a convent, bathhouses, palaces, streets with shops and ordinary homes, and the abutments of a single-arched bridge over the Arpa River. A few minutes' walk away in the gorge is an early solution to urban overcrowding – a satellite town of caves cut into the cliffs. The same high architectural standards are evident here: there is even a cave church with frescoes on its walls and ceiling.

The city's future survival

Earthquakes in 1319, 1832, and 1988, as well as blasting in a nearby quarry and even target practice by the army have all damaged the city's ancient architecture. Some ham-fisted repair work has done more harm than good. Currently, the city is on the 'at risk' register of the World Monuments Fund.

Ani's sovereignty, meanwhile, remains contested. Today the ruins sit just inside Turkey; Armenia lies a piece of rubble's throw away across a disputed frontier. Although open to visitors, it remains fenced off in a Turkish military enclave. History would suggest that this may not always remain the case. Ani may have been forgotten by the world at large for several centuries, but the Armenians have always remembered. One day they may yet reclaim their ancient city.

MANDU

Mandu ○
INDIA

DATE ABANDONED	TYPE OF PLACE	LOCATION	REASON	INHABITANTS	CURRENT STATUS
Eighteenth century	City/Fortress	India	Political	300,000	Abandoned

THIS HUGE FORTRESS TOWN WAS ONCE THE CAPITAL OF A MIGHTY MUSLIM KINGDOM. NOW, NEARLY FOUR CENTURIES AFTER IT CEASED TO BE THE PLEASURE GROUND OF EMPERORS, IT STILL POSSESSES EXQUISITE AND EXOTIC BEAUTY.

ABOVE: The Rupmati Pavilion commands princely views over the Narmada Valley.

Capital of kings

India has an abundance of romantic ruins, lost towns and derelict forts, but perhaps none of them are as magical as Mandu. It lies at the end of a dusty bus ride 100 km (62 miles) southwest of the city of Indore in the state of Madhya Pradesh. An eyrie-like plateau 300 m (990 ft) above the fertile plains of the Narmada River offers a fine defensive position and a glorious vista.

A Sanskrit inscription from AD 555 records that Mandu had already been a fortress for a thousand years. It was expanded in the tenth and eleventh centuries, but its true golden age began in the fifteenth century with the crowning of Hoshang Shah, the first Muslim king of the surrounding Malwa region. He made Mandu his capital city and a truly formidable fortress. The ridge-top plateau, which measures 10 km (6 miles) from north to south and 15 km (9 miles) from east to west, was completely ringed with a defensive wall, presenting 37 km (23 miles) of battlements to would-be conquerors. Twelve heavily built gates controlled humanity's ebb and flow. Inside the battlements, gorgeous buildings sprouted like flowers in a walled garden: mosques, palaces, Jain temples, mausoleums, and courtyards.

Hoshang Shah died in 1435 and was interred in a white marble mausoleum. His ancestors were from Afghanistan, and Hoshang's tomb is a beautiful example of their style of architecture. It is India's oldest marble building, with a shapely dome, marble latticework, handsome towers and courts with shady porticos. It's easy to see why the designers of the Taj Mahal came here to draw inspiration.

The Jahaz Mahal

Ghiyas-ud-din-Khilji ruled as sultan here from 1469 to 1500, and much of that time he devoted to the pursuit of pleasure and the arts. He built the Jahaz Mahal to house his harem, which was reputed to have numbered thousands of women. Sited between two artificial lakes, it is also known as the Ship Palace for the way it appears to float above the water in the mellow light of dawn and dusk. Its arches, galleries and domes appear as if in a dream from the *Arabian Nights*.

Keeping cool

Mandu's elevated position meant that getting water could be tricky; but the Mughal engineers were more than up to the task. They constructed a series of wells, reservoirs and conduits to bring water to where it was needed.

There are several *baolis*, or step wells, where elaborate staircases descend into cool subterranean chambers, and pools of water offer sweet refreshment from the summer heat and dust.

Rupmati's Pavilion is a large sandstone structure that was originally a military observation post. Clinging to the clifftop over a 305 m (1,000 ft) precipice, it was ingeniously supplied with water by a reservoir situated below its elevated position.

Mandu even had its own hammam, or Turkish bath house, where the sultans could steam away their stately cares.

Abandonment

The city was the king in a continent-sized game of chess played by opposing Islamic and Hindu dynasties. It frequently changed owners over the centuries until it was taken for the last time by the Hindu Marathas dynasty in 1732. However, they soon moved out, choosing the city of Dhar as their capital, and life began to drift away from Mandu.

Today a modern village, also called Mandu, lies just to the south of the ruined citadel. Its ancient heart is the huge Jama Masjid, or Friday Mosque. This is notable for its serene central courtyard and the neat ranks of red sandstone arches around the mihrab. Old Mandu may be gone, but already its seeds have grown new life.

The Jahaz Mahal, or Ship Palace, sits between two artificial lakes.

ROSS ISLAND

DATE ABANDONED	TYPE OF PLACE	LOCATION	REASON	INHABITANTS	CURRENT STATUS
1913	Explorers' base camp	Antarctica	Death	25	Preserved

THIS WAS A STOREROOM, SCIENTIFIC LABORATORY, A STABLE AND A HOME FOR TWENTY-FIVE MEN. THE HUT FROM WHICH CAPTAIN SCOTT SET OUT ON HIS FATAL JOURNEY TO THE SOUTH POLE STANDS LITERALLY FROZEN IN TIME, PRESERVED BY THE SAME SUB-ZERO CLIMATE THAT KILLED HIM.

BELOW: Abandoned crates outside Scott's Terra Nova Hut, Cape Evans.

FOLLOWING PAGE: The interior of Shackleton's Nimrod Hut has been literally frozen in time: the bedding, tinned food and even the men's socks still await them.

Antarctic basecamp, 1911

Tinned ham and whisky are stacked on the shelves beside jars of olives and anchovy paste, awaiting the return of the man who put them there. However, he never would step back into this cosy living space and enjoy the food he had left behind. His name was Robert Falcon Scott – and when he walked out of here it was to go to his doom in an Antarctic blizzard.

Scott's sensational journey

When Scott left Britain on his attempt to be first to reach the South Pole, he was already a national hero. He had commanded the National Antarctic Expedition of 1901–1904, which included another great explorer, Ernest Shackleton. Scott and Shackleton had walked further south than anyone else in history: they got to within 850 km (530 miles) of the pole.

When he announced another Antarctic expedition, hopes were high that a Briton would be the first to stand on the bottom of the world. Scott's expedition sailed from Cardiff in June 1910 on the former whaling ship, *Terra Nova*. It travelled via New Zealand and arrived at Ross Island, Antarctica in January 1911.

Ross Island is a fearsome place. Although little bigger than Anglesey, it has four huge volcanoes, two of which are over 3,048 m (10,000 ft) tall. This gives it the highest average elevation of any island in the world. The only inhabitants are half a million Adélie penguins. It is almost permanently ice-bound, shackled to the Antarctic continent by the frozen sea. However, in summer, it is reachable by boat – the most southerly such island in the world, making it an ideal base for Antarctic explorers.

As soon as they arrived, they set about erecting the prefabricated hut that would be home to twenty-five men throughout the Antarctic winter of 1911. It took a week to build the 15 m (50 ft) long and 7.6 m (25 ft) wide structure. The hut was insulated with seaweed quilt sandwiched between inner and outer double-plank walls, a design so successful that the men found it uncomfortably warm inside.

The push for the pole

With the base established, the next task was to lay caches of supplies on the route to the pole. The Antarctic summer presented a window of relatively better weather and constant light, but it only lasted from November to March. The expedition team needed as many supplies laid down in advance as possible if they were to complete the 1,450 km (900 mile) trek to the pole – and return – in that time.

However, bad weather and weak ponies meant that the main supply point, One Ton Depot, was laid 56 km (35 miles) north of its planned location. This would cost the returning party dearly.

The expedition finally departed on 1 November 1911, in a caravan of motor sledges, ponies, dogs and men. Like booster rockets on the space shuttle, one by one the support teams turned back. It was five men on foot – Scott, Wilson, Oates, Bowers and Evans – who scaled the 200 km (125 mile) long Beardmore Glacier and set out across the lifeless Antarctic plateau towards the South Pole.

'The worst has happened'

Scott and his party reached the South Pole on 17 January 1912. There they discovered that Norwegian explorer Roald Amundsen had beaten them to their great prize by five weeks. In a flag-topped tent, Amundsen had left a note to the King of Norway and a request that Scott deliver it. 'All the day dreams must go,' wrote the anguished Scott in his diary. 'Great God! This is an awful place.'

There was nothing for the distraught men to do but start the 1,300 km (800 mile) return journey. This was a savage undertaking, and the exhausted explorers were pained with frostbite and snowblindness. Edgar Evans died on 17 February after collapsing at the foot of the Beardmore Glacier.

The remaining four trekked on, but Lawrence Oates' toes had become severely frostbitten and he knew that he was holding back his colleagues. On 16 March, Scott wrote in his diary that Oates stood up, said 'I am just going outside and may be some time', then walked out of the tent and was never seen again.

On 19 March the three surviving men camped for the last time. A ferocious blizzard kept them in their tent in temperatures of -44°C, and sealed their fate. They died of starvation and exposure ten days later. They were just 18 km (11 miles) short of One Ton Depot. Scott was the last to die.

A search party found the tent eight months later. Inside were the frozen corpses along with Scott's diary. The explorers' bodies were buried under the tent and a cairn erected on top in their memory. After a century of snowstorms, the cairn and tent now lie under 23 m (75 ft) of ice. They have become part of the ice shelf, and have already moved 48 km (30 miles) from where they died. In 300 years or so the explorers will once again reach the ocean when they will drift away inside an iceberg.

Frozen in time

Scott's hut was reused by Ernest Shackleton's team in 1915–1917, but was thereafter completely abandoned until 1956, when it was dug out of the snow and ice by an American team. They found that the sub-zero weather conditions had preserved its contents almost perfectly. It's still there today, and it offers a fascinating insight into a place that is strangely familiar and yet situated in an utterly alien world.

The familiar brands show that even the boldest of Edwardian explorers loved his home comforts as much as we do: Heinz tomato ketchup (stoppered with a cork), tins of Lyle's golden syrup, Fry's cocoa and Colman's mustard.

Stoves, lights, fur-lined boots and clothes, bedding and dog harnesses all lie where the explorers left them. A corridor is still piled with cuts of seal blubber, which would have been used for cooking, heating and in lanterns. Dishes stand neatly stacked on shelves, cups hang from a row of hooks. Scott's worktable has an open book, a copy of the London Illustrated News and a stuffed Emperor penguin on it. Scientific equipment fills a workbench, and the darkroom of the expedition photographer still has its chemicals and plates. There is even the rusting frame of a bicycle and some hockey sticks – after all, these men needed some way of passing their time.

The hut must then have been a crowded, noisy and smelly place with two dozen men clustered round the table, trying to keep their bodies strong and their spirits up. It is bereft of living beings now, but there is life here all the same. One only has to look at the clothes, the maps, the lamps and the tins of sweet fruit stacked in hope for a return that never came, to feel the power of the human spirit.

Robert Falcon Scott in the Cape Evans
Hut, October 1911.

Shackleton's hut

Scott's is not the only preserved hut in the Antarctic. Ernest Shackleton's 1907–1909 Nimrod expedition fell short in its attempt on the pole, but made a successful first ascent of Mount Erebus, Antarctica's second highest volcano. Their hut on Cape Royds, 12 km (7.5 miles) from Scott's on Cape Evans, stands in a similar state of preservation.

Portraits of King Edward VII and Queen Alexandra still hang on the walls inside, and the shelves are stacked with 5,000 personal items belonging to the nine men who wintered here in 1908. Some of the 450 tins of baked beans and 540 lb of golden syrup that they brought as supplies are still stacked on the shelves.

These Antarctic huts continue to offer up surprises. In 2010, a team found two crates of brandy and three crates of whisky buried under the Nimrod hut floor. Shackleton

had originally taken 300 bottles of Mackinlay's finest malt whisky – although a teetotaller himself, he thought his men might appreciate a warming dram in the endless Antarctic night.

The legends live on

The science started by Scott's expedition is continuing even today. The readings logged by the early 20th century instruments are now being compared to current values, to help us understand the effects of climate change on Antarctica.

The buildings were given a little loving renovation in 2010. Despite the brutal environment in which they stand, they will live on a little longer as shrines to the men of the Heroic Age of Antarctic Exploration and their incredible achievements.

STELLING VAN AMSTERDAM

Stelling van Amsterdam
NETHERLANDS

DATE ABANDONED	TYPE OF PLACE	LOCATION	REASON	INHABITANTS	CURRENT STATUS
1914–1963	Defensive cordon	Netherlands	Technological redundancy	Several thousand soldiers	UNESCO World Heritage Site

DOZENS OF FORTS AND KILOMETRES OF MOATS CREATED AN IMPREGNABLE BARRIER OF WATER AND CONCRETE AROUND AMSTERDAM. IT WOULD BE UNDONE AND ITS WALLS DESERTED NOT BY THE POUNDING OF HEAVY ARTILLERY, BUT BY THE INVENTION OF FLIGHT.

State of the military art

The Stelling van Amsterdam was the most advanced military structure of its type in the world – 135 km (84 miles) of forts, batteries and moats completely encircling the city in a defensive barrier. Nearly half a century in the making, the colossal defensive system was staffed by thousands of soldiers. Yet it would be abandoned by almost all of them, almost overnight – not because an enemy had somehow overcome its concrete walls and bristling artillery, but because inventions in a field of combat far from here made all its brilliance count for nothing.

War on the doorstep

In the late nineteenth century there were three constantly clashing superpowers triangulated around the Netherlands: France, Germany and the United Kingdom. This was a time of Empire when the reward for control of the sea was nothing less than world dominion. The Netherlands was an exposed place to be.

The Franco-Prussian War of 1870–1 saw the introduction of new, more powerful artillery. The Dutch Ministry of War rightly judged that their existing defences would be vulnerable against these modern weapons. In 1874 a bold new concept was approved: a defensive belt of fortifications around Amsterdam.

The initial concept was to create a defensive moat 10–15 km (6–9 miles) out from the city centre, turning Amsterdam's low-lying coastal position into a defensive boon. In the event of enemy attack, sluices would be opened to inundate wide areas of flat farmland with water. The flooding would be no more than 30 cm (12 inches) deep – too shallow for enemy boats to cross; deep enough to hinder men on foot.

The obvious weak points would be the roads, railways, and dykes that ran through the inundations; raised from the land, these would still be usable even after flooding. So forts would be built where these routes crossed the

A circular tower fort, still surrounded by its moat, by the River Vecht.

waterline, to be armed with powerful artillery ready to shell the approaching foe.

The first setback
The first design became obsolete while still on the drawing board. Another innovation in warfare – the high explosive grenade – meant that the forts would have to be built of concrete rather than masonry. The Dutch were inexperienced in using concrete and had to undertake years of research and development.

Construction itself was a vast undertaking. As well as forty-six fortifications, there were numerous smaller batteries, depots and barracks, as well as a huge network of sluices, dykes, canals and artificial islands to be constructed. When flooded, the inundations were designed to be 3–5 km (1.9–3 miles) wide. The project took almost forty years to complete, from 1881 to 1920.

Completion and redundancy
No sooner was this mammoth construction project complete than it was rendered instantly obsolete by two military innovations – the aeroplane and the tank. Planes could simply fly over the forts to drop bombs on the city itself. Tanks could roll through the inundations and were unlikely to be deterred by the artillery in the forts.

Soldiers manned the Stelling during both World Wars, but its ingenuity was never tested in combat. However, it was methodically maintained and kept in service until 1963, when it was decommissioned. Now abandoned as a military resource, its structures are an interesting insight into the Europe of 150 years ago. They also showcase the Dutch genius for hydraulic engineering.

A city wall of water and guns
The Stelling is a fascinating place to explore. Many of the forts are open to visitors, and some have been preserved exactly as they were when the last soldiers left. Some are now surrounded by suburbs and can be easily reached by foot or bicycle; others stand guarding the cows in low-lying farmland. There is a hiking route that runs the full 135 km (84 miles) around the original defence line, although the island forts must be reached by ferry or private vessel.

The fact that the Stelling never was attacked has ensured the survival of many of its most spectacular fortifications. Pampus Fort stands on an artificial island of 45,000 cubic metres of sand supported by 3,800 deeply sunk piles. The three-floor main building is surrounded by a dry moat 8 m (26 ft) wide and has two turrets that each held twin 57 mm (2.2 inch) guns. Within are quarters for 200 soldiers, a kitchen, laundry and classrooms, two coal-fired steam engines, two dynamos, a telegraph, a first aid station and magazines. Tunnels connect the building to galleries inside the *counterscarp*, or outside of the moat, where defenders could fire four M90 Gardner machine guns on attackers who made it into the moat. Also within the counterscarp were a jail, a forge, and several supply rooms. A large *glacis*, or artificial slope, surrounds the fort on all sides.

There were originally eighty-seven polders ready to be inundated by military waterworks, and today thirty-five of these sluice systems remain. The inundation station at Schagen was typical of the Dutch mastery of water. It drew water in from the North Sea and guided it southwards to the next station in the defence line at Krommeniedijk.

Had there been no major advances in military technology, the Stelling van Amsterdam would have been one of the world's most prodigious defences. There were such advances, of course, and today the system stands as a monumental military idea, abandoned when a new strategy was made necessary.

The fort island of IJmuiden on the North Sea Canal was adapted to form part of Hitler's Atlantic Wall. This 2,685 km (1,670 mile) long defensive system was built by the Germans along Europe's Atlantic coast to prevent an Allied invasion.

KAYAKÖY

TURKEY
Kayaköy

DATE ABANDONED	TYPE OF PLACE	LOCATION	REASON	INHABITANTS	CURRENT STATUS
1923	Town	Turkey	Political	2,000	Preserved

CAUGHT ON THE WRONG SIDE OF A SHIFTING BORDER DISPUTED BY WARRING NATIONS, THE POPULATION OF KAYAKÖY WAS EVICTED WHOLESALE AND AGAINST THEIR WISHES IN AN ACT OF ETHNIC CLEANSING.

Peace among the ruins

In the ninety years since these houses were abandoned their rafters and doors have been stripped by human hands and nature's powers, leaving only walls and chimneys standing proud of the rubble. However, despite the desolation, this is a very peaceful and enchanting place. Grassy streets run between the hundreds of crumbling hovels. Simple churches offer sanctuary from the burning sun. Olive trees flourish in the echoing town square. In spring, wildflowers add a splash of sweet melancholy to the ruins. Above it all rise the sleepy green hills which seem to hold the village in an embrace.

Kayaköy is a peaceful place to wander through, but this quiet serenity belies the fact that the town as it is today was born from vicious ethnic violence.

Trading places

Kayaköy was founded as the Greek village of Levissi in the eighteenth century. Its population surged after the nearby village of Fethiye was shattered by an earthquake in 1856. Levissi became a centre of Greek Orthodox worship with more than twenty churches and chapels built in the village and on the surrounding plain.

At the end of the First World War, the victorious Allies promised Greece territory that had been held by the Ottoman Empire. In 1919, Greek forces set out to seize these lands, occupying Smyrna and several other cities in Anatolia (the Asian part of Turkey).

However, the Greek army was eventually defeated by Turkish forces and the disputed territory was incorporated into the Republic of Turkey. There was then a population exchange between the two countries: Greeks living in Turkish territory returned to Greece and vice versa. The numbers were huge – at least a million Greeks made the move and 500,000 Muslims were displaced from the Greek territories. The wholly Greek town of Kayaköy was left deserted when its population was forcibly sent to a motherland that the people barely knew.

The spiritual atmosphere amid the stones

As well as its atmospheric, tumbledown houses, Kayaköy has several interesting historic sites. A handful of buildings have been restored and one is home to a small museum that explains the history of the settlement. There is a splendid fountain in the middle of the town and two notable Greek Orthodox churches. Known as the

Inside the Upper Church.

The scattering of roofless houses seen from above.

The Lower Church was at
the heart of the town.

Lower and the Upper Churches, these are small and built in a seventeenth century gothic style.

The Lower Church is the better preserved, with traces of blue and gold on its altar. Crowning the highest hill in the town is the Upper Church, the older of the two. Outside the building, the mosaic courtyard is still in remarkably good condition. Inside, the church presents a very poetic picture of decay. Scattered holes in the roof let in shafts of sunlight, illuminating the interior as if to suggest that somebody up there still cares about this place.

SONARGAON

BANGLADESH
Sonargaon

DATE ABANDONED	TYPE OF PLACE	LOCATION	REASON	INHABITANTS	CURRENT STATUS
Twentieth century	City	Bangladesh	Economic/ Religious	Thousands at its peak	Gradual decay

A RICH TRADING CENTRE PRIZED BY HINDU, ISLAMIC, MUGHAL, AND BRITISH EMPIRES IS NOW SLOWLY BEING WASHED AWAY BY AN INDIFFERENT CLIMATE. SOME OF THE OLDEST BUILDINGS IN BANGLADESH ARE ALL BUT LOST AMID THE RAINS AND THE FLOURISHING JUNGLE.

The town of many empires

It is only 24 km (15 miles) from the hive-like hubbub of Bangladesh's capital city, Dhaka, but Sonargaon feels like it exists on a different planet. It was a Hindu trading outpost by the thirteenth century and it later became an Islamic spiritual retreat. As seagoing international trade increased from the fourteenth century onwards, Sonargaon steadily grew in size and influence.

It boomed again under British colonial rule, with the establishment of the textile-producing neighbourhood of Panam City. Street after street of elegant Indo-European townhouses were built in the late 1800s to house a prosperous new population of upper-middle class Bengali businessmen.

Left behind in a new age

British rule officially ended in 1947, and the former empire was divided along religious lines: India (Hindu) and Pakistan (Muslim). As Sonargaon became part of East Pakistan, many of its Hindu residents fled across the border to India. Bangladesh was established as an independent country in 1971 at the end of a fierce civil war. By that time this once affluent town had been abandoned, with most of its remaining inhabitants having moved to the growing city of Dhaka.

Today the old town is recognized as being at risk and is officially protected. However, the damp climate, lack of maintenance and infestation with woodworm and other pests are all causing visible damage to the buildings. Spacious rooms ringed with elegant arches, where the floors were once covered in bolts of golden cloth, are now home only to puddles and damp stone. Carved stone balustrades writhe with vines and the once airy balconies are choked with young forest. Where roofs have tumbled in, the walls are often slick with running rainwater, which washes away a little more plaster here, a little more there.

Perhaps a new influx of tourists will bring in the money the town needs to preserve its architectural treasures, but it's hard to imagine this happening. This is a land where mere survival can be difficult enough: 80 per cent of Bangladesh is flood plain and the country is prone to flooding from the annual monsoons and frequent cyclones. Change here is rapid and ruthless, and it may have irreversibly made its home in the streets of Sonargaon.

The only resident in a street that once housed hundreds.

ST KILDA

DATE ABANDONED	TYPE OF PLACE	LOCATION	REASON	INHABITANTS	CURRENT STATUS
29 August 1930	Island community	Hebrides, Scotland	Hardship	36	UNESCO World Heritage Site/Military base

FOR 2,000 YEARS, A SMALL COMMUNITY LIVED ON AN ISLAND THAT WAS PART OF BRITAIN YET UTTERLY ALIEN TO IT. AS THE TWENTIETH CENTURY CAME KNOCKING, THEIR ANCIENT, MONEYLESS WAY OF LIFE SIMPLY BECAME TOO DIFFICULT COMPARED WITH WHAT WAS AVAILABLE ELSEWHERE.

ABOVE: The steep cliffs of St Kilda are home to the largest colony of gannets in Europe. There are more than 60,000 nests.

The island on the edge of the world

'And I am come down to deliver them … and to bring them up out of that land unto a good land and a large, unto a land flowing with milk and honey …'
The Book of Exodus

The minister finished his reading and left the Bible open on its simple wooden lectern. The people briefly returned to their houses to place small piles of oats in their hearths as tokens of faith, or gratitude. Then they gathered up the last of their belongings and let the minister lead them down to the jetty. There they boarded the ship that would take them away from the only home that they had ever known, and bring two millennia of human habitation on St Kilda to an end.

The westernmost isle

The archipelago of St Kilda is not just wild, it is beyond the horizon. Although part of the United Kingdom, it never appears in any road atlas. Firstly, that's because it has no roads; but it also lies 64 km (40 miles) out into the Atlantic Ocean off the westernmost point of Scotland's Outer Hebrides. It is by far the most remote part of the British Isles ever to be anyone's home.

The largest island of the group, and the only one ever to be inhabited, is Hirta, which also has some of the highest sea cliffs in the United Kingdom. There are three other islands: Dun, Soay and Boreray, and several spiky sea stacks rising like giant canines from the heaving swell.

A communal way of life

The islands were first inhabited during the Bronze Age and supported a population of up to 180 for much of that time. The St Kildans originally spoke Gaelic, not English, and were clothed in a similar style to people in the Outer Hebrides.

The islanders lived in various types of dwelling over the years, some of which remain. The crescent of cottages that we see today was built in the 1830s. Originally they were Hebridean black houses with a single room in which the cattle also slept in winter. Each house had its own strip of land for growing crops. New houses, which boasted a second room, were built in the 1860s.

There is only a little arable land, but there is an almost limitless supply of seabirds. The men would meet in a daily parliament to decide which tasks needed to be done and who would do them. Usually, this meant most of the men scaling the dizzy cliffs and collecting the birds by snare, fowling rod or by hand. Puffins, fulmars and gannets were the most commonly eaten birds, and their feathers and oil were also put to good use. Other jobs included mending fishing nets or collecting sheep from the outlying islands in a small boat.

Life was simple. It has been estimated that each person on St Kilda ate 115 fulmars every year. Puffins were a favourite snack. Food was unvarying, but it was nutritious and plentiful; the islanders did not starve. Every haul of eggs, fish and seabirds was divided out equally amongst the villagers. There was no need for money.

For centuries the only contact with the outside world were the occasional visits of whaling and fishing boats, and the annual visit of the rent collector. The islanders rented St Kilda from the Macleods of Dunvegan in Skye – a far-off landlord. As the islanders had no money, the Macleods' rent collector accepted payment in oats, barley, fish, cattle and sheep products, and seabirds. He would also trade in goods that the islanders couldn't make, such as tools and homewares. The rent collector was accompanied by a minister who performed any baptisms and weddings that had become necessary in the previous year.

As more frequent communication became established, the church on the mainland began to send ministers out more often. A church and manse were built in the early nineteenth century and a minister moved in full time. A school was added in 1884.

Oppressed by religion

A visitor in 1697, Martin Martin, noted that the people loved to play games and make music. However, the Victorian tourists often commented on how sad the people seemed. As if life here wasn't tough enough, the minister who came in 1865 seems to have been a 'fire-and-brimstone' merchant of the first order, who ruled the people with a cross of iron.

He made attendance compulsory at three Sunday services, each two or three hours long. When a boat bringing vital food to relieve a near-famine arrived one Saturday, the minister told the skipper he must not unload the supplies until Monday: the islanders had to prepare for the Sabbath. The island's children were banned from playing games, and had to carry a bible with them at all times. So much time was spent in observation of religious matters that practical matters became neglected.

'The Sabbath was a day of intolerable gloom. At the clink of the bell the whole flock hurry to Church with sorrowful looks and eyes bent upon the ground. It is considered sinful to look to the right or to the left.'
A visitor in 1875

First contact with the wider world

The steam yacht *Vulcan* visited St Kilda in 1838. This was one of the first meetings between ordinary British people from the mainland and the islanders, but such interactions would soon become common. Victorians were fascinated by what they regarded as a primitive people living at the very edge of Britain, the most civilized nation on earth.

This was a defining time in their history: before then, the outside world must have seemed alien and unattractive to the St Kildans, if not downright terrifying. Now they had a greater understanding of what it could offer; particularly how much more comfort it was possible for people to enjoy.

Some inhabitants decided to make a complete break. In 1852, thirty-six – more than one third of the island's population at the time – sailed for Australia. The ones who survived the arduous journey settled in Melbourne, where they named the suburb of St Kilda after their home island.

In 1877 regular summer cruises took curious tourists out to see the St Kildans. By 1889 the islanders were spending much of their time making things that they could sell to the visitors: tweeds, gloves, stockings, scarves and sheepskins. They also sold many of the birds' eggs that they collected.

This brought them new clothes, equipment and food, but it also destroyed their self-sufficiency. They came to depend

on imported fuel, provisions and building materials. It wasn't just skills they lost, but also the will to continue making the huge effort necessary to live on St Kilda; their morale was waning.

The lack of regular communication with the rest of Scotland led to some trying times. A food shortage in 1876 got so bad that the islanders had to call for help. The only method open to them was sending out a message in bottle: a letter begging for food was sealed in a small wooden casket and a sheep's bladder attached to act as a float. This was then launched into the waves in the hope that it would wash up on the mainland, and be found, before the situation got too much worse.

There was another famine in 1912 and the following year influenza savaged the islanders. The First World War might have seemed remote, but it affected even this lonely island. The islands were in a strategically useful position, and a naval detachment came to the island to run a signal station. Their presence meant frequent landings of mail and food. Unlike nearly everyone else in Europe, for the St Kildans the war was a time of certainty, security and relative plenty.

At the conflict's end the regular deliveries dried up. It must have laid a heavy sense of isolation on the islanders, because most of the able-bodied young islanders emigrated. There were 73 islanders in 1920; by 1928 there were only 37. The years of regular communication with the mainland had shown them that there was an alternative, easier, life to be had there. The island's once smoothly functioning society was irreparably broken; its days were numbered.

Influenza returned in 1926, killing four men, and there were frequent famines from crop failures throughout the 1920s. When a pregnant woman died from appendicitis in January 1930, after being unable to be evacuated due to bad weather, the islanders had had enough. The thirty-six remaining islanders unanimously decided to leave and asked the British Government for homes on the mainland. On 29 August 1930, two millennia of human habitation on St Kilda came to an end.

Most of the refugees who left here in 1930 settled in Argyll. The younger men were given forestry jobs, which was a strange choice, as most of them had never seen a tree.

Exploring today

The entire archipelago is now owned by the National Trust for Scotland. It is a World Heritage Site and one of the few places to be so honoured both for its natural and its cultural qualities. There has also been a missile tracking station here since 1955, which brought with it a few permanent military residents. Several conservation workers and scientists come to stay every summer.

There are no ferries to St Kilda, so visiting is a matter of hiring a vessel and a skipper. The journey over in a little boat can be 'lumpy' (as one captain memorably described some enormous waves) but it makes the arrival all the more impressive.

As the islands get close it becomes clear how enormous the cliffs are. The huge sea stacks erupt sheer out of the waves and tower endlessly above you. It's as if the great crags of Ben Nevis had been scooped up and dropped into the ocean. The cliff face of Conachair rises 427 m (1,401 ft) straight up out of the waves.

All the time the puffins and gulls wheel and swarm above the boat in a kaleidoscope of coloured feathers. The noise of their thousands is multiplied into a cacophony by the rock walls.

The village itself is modest, lying in an arc of flat land between two curving rock headlands, as if being embraced by the island itself. It has just one street, with a dozen or so single-storey stone cottages facing the endless sea. A cluster of stone sheep-folds and the tiny jetty are just about the only other structures here.

One thing the island does have in abundance is peace. Standing here past the far west of our everyday world as the sun sets further west still, it is plain to see how hard it was to live here; but also, how hard it must have been to leave.

Sixteen new two-room cottages were built in 1860; they are now mostly roofless shells.

BOKOR HILL STATION

CAMBODIA

○ Bokor Hill Station

DATE ABANDONED	TYPE OF PLACE	LOCATION	REASON	INHABITANTS	CURRENT STATUS
1940s	Colonial resort	Cambodia	Political	Seasonal guests and staff	Abandoned

LOST IN THE MOUNTAIN MISTS IS A HILLTOP REFUGE OF INDOCHINA'S COLONIAL OVERLORDS. ITS RUINED CASINO, BALLROOM AND APARTMENTS OFFER A GLIMPSE BACK IN TIME TO A VERY DIFFERENT ERA OF SOUTHEAST ASIA'S HISTORY.

Ghosts on the mountaintop

When the mists shroud Bokor Hill Station, which they frequently do, the decaying buildings take on an almost supernatural aura. The balconies built for views of the plains far below now look out into a spectral grey emptiness and the silence in the long-empty rooms becomes almost palpable. It's easy then to imagine the elegant, dinner-jacketed ghosts of the colonists who built this little outpost of French civilization in the forested wilds of Cambodia.

The cool retreat in the hills

Cambodia became a French protectorate in 1867, and then part of French Indochina, a federation of colonies that included territory in Vietnam and Laos.

Phnom Penh may have been known as the 'Pearl of Asia' for its beauty, but it was also hot, humid and full of the noise and dirt of a capital city. For half the year it was deluged by torrential rain. The colonial French settlers wanted a bolthole in the hills where they could enjoy a more temperate climate, much as the British had at Darjeeling in India.

Bokor Hill was built as just such a resort in 1921. Perched on a mountain-edge at a lofty 1,048 m (3,438 ft), the site offered spellbinding views to the Gulf of Thailand. The resort's largest and most magnificent building was the grand Bokor Palace Hotel and Casino. There

were also shops, a post office, a Catholic church and the grandly named Royal Apartments.

However, the mountain is remote and the surrounding landscape is unforgiving: 900 workers died during construction of the resort.

The empire crumbles

Colonial rule in Cambodia was interrupted during the Second World War; France itself was invaded by Germany in 1940 putting it in no position to defend its colonies. Despite General Charles de Gaulle's determination to re-establish French Indochina after the war, Cambodia moved ever closer to independence, which it finally won in 1953.

The French left Bokor Hill during the war and never came back. It was then occupied by various local anti-French resistance groups before being taken over by the Khmer Rouge, the ruling party in Cambodia from 1975 to 1979. In 1979 the Khmer Rouge used it as a military fortification, holding out in the former casino against the invading Vietnamese forces. The brutal regime was ousted from power, but a pocket of Khmer Rouge fighters kept possession of Bokor until the early 1990s. Since then it has been completely abandoned.

The site is government-owned but has been leased to a development group, which plans to repair the old hotel and casino and add new restaurants and a golf course to resurrect Bokor as a resort. However, at the current time this plan has not advanced and the buildings are still in a derelict state.

RED SANDS SEA FORTS

UNITED KINGDOM

Red Sands Sea Forts ○

DATE ABANDONED	TYPE OF PLACE	LOCATION	REASON	INHABITANTS	CURRENT STATUS
1943	Military fortification	Thames Estuary, UK	War	Up to 265	Ruined

WHEN HITLER'S LUFTWAFFE TARGETTED SHIPPING IN THE RIVER THAMES DURING THE SECOND WORLD WAR, THE ADMIRALTY CREATED AN EXTRAORDINARY UNIT OF OFFSHORE ANTI-AIRCRAFT FORTS. IN THE 1960s THE DECOMMISSIONED STRUCTURES BECAME HIDEOUTS FOR PIRATE RADIO STATIONS BEFORE BEING LEFT TO THE MERCY OF THE SEA.

ABOVE: Red Sands Sea Forts in the Thames estuary, now abandoned. The Kentish Flats windfarm is just behind on the horizon.

Stalkers of the sea

They look like one of H. G. Wells' most fantastical creations come to life: four-legged, fat-bodied metal monsters striding in formation through the waves off the English coast. But these sea-bound structures are not invaders: they were actually a vital part of Britain's coastal defences in the Second World War.

They would also have been a prime contender for the title of strangest street in Britain. For here 265 men lived in seven interlinked houses, each measuring just 11 m (36 ft) square and completely surrounded by the cold, black waters of the North Sea.

Innovation in offshore defence

London's docks were the busiest in the world in 1939. They were the trade hub of the British Empire and a conduit for one third of the country's imports and exports, handling 35 million tonnes of cargo per year. More than 100,000 dockers, stevedores and sailors bustled around 1700 wharves. The outbreak of the Second World War made the docks – and the Thames shipping routes – imperative targets for German bombs.

With the war under way, German aircraft laid thousands of magnetic mines in British waters. Over 100 British ships were sunk in the Thames estuary alone in the early months of the war. The Thames urgently needed anti-aircraft defences and the Admiralty asked engineer Guy Maunsell to help. He designed two types of fort, the Navy and the Army styles.

An 'Army fort' comprised a group of seven 4-legged towers connected by tubular steel walkways. These structures were built in Gravesend, towed down-river and then carefully sunk onto the seabed between May and December 1943. There were three Army forts: Nore, Shivering Sands and this one at Red Sands.

Each tower had a two-storey structure for living and working, with differing artillery or other equipment on the roof: one tower had two 40 mm Bofors medium anti-aircraft guns, four towers had 3.7-inch heavy anti-aircraft guns, one tower had a searchlight and there was also a central control tower with radar.

The forts were not a popular posting among soldiers. As well as being cold, windy, damp and isolated places to live, the towers were very vulnerable to enemy attack. Being metal towers amid an open sea also made them extremely good lightning conductors. Even on non-stormy days static electricity would build up to such an extent that soldiers who touched metal door handles would be thrown across the room.

Nevertheless, the Thames forts were a success. Their searchlights picked out hundreds of approaching aircraft and their guns downed twenty-two planes, over thirty flying bombs and accounted for one U-boat. They were maintained for a decade after the war ended, but in 1956 their guns were removed and they were left to the mercy of the North Sea. They would probably all have been allowed to rust into oblivion were it not for some very unlikely new tenants: rock-and-roll radio outlaws.

Ruling the airwaves

In 1964, a new era in broadcasting was launched from a ship moored outside UK territorial waters: Radio Caroline. This pioneering pirate radio venture inspired promoter and personality Screaming Lord Sutch to set up 'Radio Sutch' in one of the Shivering Sands towers a few months later. For the next few years the venture flourished, taking over the four other towers that were still connected by walkways, and becoming known as Radio City. Red Sands was also occupied by a pirate broadcaster: Radio Invicta, later named Radio 390.

The Army forts were ideal for pirate radio broadcasting in their form as well as their location. A large antenna could be placed on the central tower and then guyed to the surrounding towers. They had also been designed for habitation, however rudimentary.

The pirates were outlawed for good in 1967 and formally evicted; but there would be one final offshore resident.

The Principality of Sealand

Paddy Roy Bates was an ex-British Army major and pirate radio broadcaster. When offshore broadcasting was outlawed in 1967 he moved into Roughs Tower, a Maunsell fort of the Navy design. He then declared this to be the 'Principality of Sealand', the world's smallest independent country, and himself to be its prince. 'Prince Roy' created a constitution, a national anthem and a flag, and he issued passports. The Royal Navy tried to close him down, but their case was thrown out in court: the judge ruled that Britain had no territorial right over Sealand. Thereafter Bates was left to pursue his eccentric vision of nationhood more or less unmolested.

INSETS RIGHT: A few military furnishings still lie inside today.
BELOW RIGHT: A supply boat arrives at the active forts.

Red Sands today

The Nore group of towers was considered a shipping hazard and was completely demolished in 1959. A ship crashed into one of the Shivering Sands towers in 1963, knocking it into the sea. That leaves Red Sands Fort as the only complete set of Maunsell Army towers still standing.

The first difficulty faced by would-be visitors to Red Sands Fort is that of simply finding the place: the fort stands 10 km (6 miles) offshore from Minster on the Isle of Sheppey. That accomplished, the heaving sea makes getting a boat in close a highly risky endeavour. On approach the image of giant stalking machines is even more powerful as the towers dominate any craft. The tower 'bodies' are all rusted a violent red all over, with the occasional daub of white paint picking out the slogan of a long-defunct radio station.

The sea-level ladders and walkways that soldiers once used to access the towers are now rusted to the point of uselessness, with the brine-rotted metal crumbling to the touch. However, a few visitors have managed to climb inside and they have reported a fascinating window into Britain's wartime past.

The cell-like iron rooms are still cluttered with rusted generators, the remains of radar equipment and steel-legged tables where enemy aircraft movements were plotted. There are bookshelves for charts and logbooks, and a cast-iron enamelled bath in which soldiers must have once sat and washed themselves while staring out of the window at the endless sea. From the roof it is easy to see how the seven towers would once have linked up so neatly, and how impressively exact their construction was in such an incredibly difficult environment.

In 1944 this spot would have been the centre of a blazing cacophony of gunfire, with men yelling and machinery clanking. Now the only sound is the slap of the waves, the odd seabird and the clanging of the bell in the nearby buoy that marks the edge of the shipping channel.

BODIE

DATE ABANDONED	TYPE OF PLACE	LOCATION	REASON	INHABITANTS	CURRENT STATUS
1943	Gold mining town	California	Economic	8,000	Preserved decay

GUNFIGHTERS, GOLD NUGGETS, RAILROADS, OUTLAWS, SALOONS, DANCING GIRLS – IN JUST A FEW YEARS THIS TOWN HAD EVERYTHING THAT MADE THE WEST WILD. THEN, IN THE SPACE OF ANOTHER FEW, IT LOST IT ALL.

Boom and bust in the wild, wild West

Willam S. Bodey came all the way from Poughkeepsie, New York to strike it rich. In 1848 he left his wife Sarah and his two children behind and took a boat around the Horn, arriving in San Francisco along with 300,000 other would-be gold miners.

Unlike the majority of the '49ers (as the prospectors who took part in the gold rush of 1849 were known), Bodey actually did strike gold. Ten years after he landed in California he got lucky in the scrubby hills north of Mono Lake. A gold rush started following his claim and the town named after him sprang into existence. Bodey himself saw none of its wealth – he froze to death in a blizzard just months after his big discovery.

After a slow start, the town of Bodie really hit pay dirt in 1876. A rich new seam of gold ore transformed Bodie from an isolated backwater camp into a virtual metropolis. California and Nevada newspapers billed the town as the next

BOTTOM LEFT: Looking east from the cemetery in the 1890s.

BOTTOM RIGHT: The wooden buildings huddle together in the lee of the mountain.

Comstock Lode – where a huge discovery of silver and gold ore had created immense fortunes. Soon there were 8,000 people living and working in 2,000 buildings.

Bodie epitomized the 'Wild West' town. Its mile-long main street had a Wells Fargo Bank, a jail and sixty-five saloons. Every night the miners and ore workers rushed into town to drink their pay. The air ran with the sound of gunfire as brawls spilled onto the streets and men died in shootouts at noon. Stagecoach holdups were so regular that armed guards soon accompanied the shipments of bullion from the town. Bodie had a thriving cluster of brothels, a railroad, a telegraph station, several daily newspapers and its own Chinatown complete with a Taoist temple and opium dens. The town had nine stamp mills, where ore was crushed for processing. There was a cemetery and even a separate Boot Hill – the graveyard for those who had died with their boots on, i.e. violently.

Mining in Bodie reached its peak in 1881 when ore worth $3.1 million was dug out of the scrubby hills. However, within just a few years it was clear that the seams in the area were fast being worked out. New strikes in Butte, Montana, and Tombstone, Arizona, began to lure the professional miners away with the promise of new bonanzas.

There were still several thousand inhabitants and several working mines at the turn of the century, but by 1910 there were only 698 people left in Bodie, most of them families who had decided to make a go of living in this remote corner. It was a brave stand, but it wasn't to last.

Only $6,821 of gold was mined in 1914. Three years later the railway was scrapped. A couple of mines limped on for a while but the last pickaxe was swung there in 1942, and the handful of remaining residents departed soon after.

The stage is still set
Most visitors remark how much Bodie looks like a movie set. Very few abandoned places can claim to have a whole cultural genre based around their heyday, but Bodie can. The characters, landscapes and architecture of the 'Western' are so familiar to most of us that one almost expects Gary Cooper or Clint Eastwood to step jingling from the saloon. After a little exploration, however, it slowly dawns that, of course, movie sets look like Bodie. This is not a plywood reconstruction, but the real thing, where people lived, worked and died.

The humanity of some abandoned places can seem remote, almost abstract, but Bodie is so real in its dereliction that it almost feels like a person itself. The buildings are scattered around the landscape, many of them sulking in hollows like children denied a treat. It's easy to imagine how each individual prospector arrived and grabbed his own little patch, then defended it dearly. It must have been hard to be a good neighbour in a town where it might be the fella next door who bags the bonanza while all you ever dig up is dirt.

Today there are just over 100 buildings still standing, left as they were when the inhabitants headed to pastures new. A Methodist church was built in 1882 and still waits for the faithful today. As families followed the single men to Bodie the wildness of the town was tempered a little. A Roman Catholic church was built the same year, but that burned down in 1930.

The cemetery has about eighty gravestones, and many of the inscriptions can still be easily read. A few have been worn down by the harsh Bodie winters; as those who sleep beneath the stones were worn down too.

The abandoned cars lying around Bodie stem from its popularity as a ghost town – it was billed as such a century before this book was written, in 1915. As motoring increased in popularity, sightseers drove out to see this strange relic of a past that wasn't all that distant but must certainly have seemed so when viewed from the leather seats of a Chrysler Imperial limousine. Many of these vehicles never made it home again, the rough roads, baking summer days and freezing nights taking their toll on the rudimentary automobiles. Perhaps a few even fell victim to aged gunslingers.

TYNEHAM

DATE ABANDONED	TYPE OF PLACE	LOCATION	REASON	INHABITANTS	CURRENT STATUS
1943	Village	Dorset, England	War	225	In military use

WITH ALLIED FORCES GEARING UP FOR D-DAY, A PRETTY LITTLE VILLAGE ON THE DORSET COAST WAS EVACUATED – TEMPORARILY – AS PART OF THE WAR EFFORT. OVER SEVENTY YEARS LATER, STILL NO ONE LIVES THERE.

Land of the army

By the time the Second World War broke out in 1939, the residents of Tyneham were accustomed to the presence of the army. Soldiers need somewhere to train for war, and Dorset's rolling chalkland offered the perfect landscape and location. The War Office first established infantry camps in nearby Bovington and Lulworth in 1899. In 1917 the area became a tank training area, and it has been home to armoured fighting vehicles ever since.

As tanks became more powerful, the army needed more space to test them and to train their operators, and the camp at Bovington expanded over the neighbouring farmland. Lulworth expanded to encompass several live firing ranges. Tyneham soon found itself in the middle of a heavy artillery practice area.

The final nail in Tyneham's coffin was the operation that would ultimately help win the war in Europe: D-Day.

Rehearsing an invasion

This do-or-die invasion of German-held continental Europe would include the greatest amphibious assault the world had ever seen, on 6 June 1944. Following that would come a flow of three million men and thousands of guns, planes and tanks from Britain into France.

The vast fighting force had to be trained in what to expect when they crossed the Channel and faced the enemy. Dozens of training camps were set up throughout Britain on beaches and inland, and activity was ramped up at existing sites such as Bovington.

On 17 November 1943, Tyneham's 225 residents received a letter from the War Office. This was an order to evacuate their homes by 19 December – just over one month away – because their village was being commandeered in 'the national interest'.

For the good of the country

The residents' first reaction was despair; many families had lived there for several generations. But, eventually, the mood softened. There was a sense that they were making a sacrifice that only they were able to make, for the good of the country. If Londoners could stand months of bombs dropping daily in the Blitz, then the people of Tyneham would endure as well.

By the time the people of Britain were making the best of Christmas 1943, Tyneham was not

only deserted, it had literally vanished off the map. Before the people of Tyneham left their homes, a resident pinned a letter to the door of St. Mary's church:

'Please treat the church and houses with care; we have given up our homes where many of us lived for generations to help win the war to keep men free. We shall return one day and thank you for treating the village kindly.'

The War Office said that the residents would be free to return when the war was over, but no one would ever call this village home again.

You can never go back

When the war ended, most of the Tyneham evictees were living in newly built homes in Wareham. Many of them were enjoying electricity and running water in their homes for the first time and had no intention of going back. Several others yearned to return and when the government issued a compulsory purchase order in 1948 to keep the land in military hands, protests erupted.

However, no matter how much people wanted to return, the army still needed somewhere to train its tank groups. Furthermore, the village was looking increasingly derelict and many former homes were uninhabitable. In 1967 the Elizabethan manor house was demolished. Most cottages and farms, as well as the post office and rectory, were roofless shells. The protests were dismissed and Tyneham has remained military property ever since.

Relic of resistance

For most of the year, Tyneham is still very much the province of the British Army. The Lulworth Ranges are the training area for the Armoured Fighting Vehicles Gunnery School. However, in 1975, the Ministry of Defence began opening the village and footpaths across the ranges at weekends and throughout August. Four years later the first church service held at Tyneham for 36 years took place.

The vales and woods may be dotted with bombed out tanks, but wildlife is flourishing here free from the intrusion of farming or housing developments. Whereas many parts of the Dorset coast have become tourism hotspots with hotels, cafés and caravan parks, Tyneham and the nearby fishing hamlet of Worbarrow Bay are among the most tranquil and isolated spots in the whole region.

The school and St Mary's Church have been preserved as living museums to the sacrifice made by this small village. Hardly anyone had heard of Tyneham before 1943; those who visit today are never likely to forget the story of this small town's sacrifice.

ORADOUR-SUR-GLANE

FRANCE
Oradour-sur-Glane

DATE ABANDONED	TYPE OF PLACE	LOCATION	REASON	INHABITANTS	CURRENT STATUS
10 June 1944	Village	France	War crime	660	Preserved as a memorial

ALL THE FURY AND SAVAGERY OF THE SECOND WORLD WAR WAS ACTED OUT IN MINIATURE IN THIS TINY RURAL FRENCH TOWN. ALMOST THE ENTIRE POPULATION WAS KILLED AND EVERY BUILDING BURNT INTO RUIN ON THE ORDERS OF A ROGUE SS COMMANDER IN A SINGLE SUMMER AFTERNOON.

Most of the houses are empty shells, as seen in this aerial image.

Carnage in a country village

Of all the world's ghost towns perhaps none has as many ghosts as Oradour-sur-Glane. For it was here that a German *Waffen*-SS company killed 642 innocent men, women and children in the most horrible manner, as a bloody example to local Resistance fighters.

Before the Second World War, Oradour-sur-Glane was the epitome of a sleepy rural town in the Haute Vienne department in France's Limousin region. It didn't have much, just an *hôtel de ville* (town hall), a church, a market, some shops and four small schools. The most modern thing about Oradour was the rickety electric tram that ran to Limoges, a town 24 km (15 miles) to the southeast.

In 1944, the town lay in what was then Vichy France. After overrunning France in 1940, Germany had carved the country up into zones. The north, including Paris, was German-occupied territory. Alsace-Lorraine, in the east, was annexed. The area around Marseille was handed to Italy almost as a gift. Much of the south was nominally self-governed from the spa town of Vichy.

From 1940–2, active opposition to German control had been sporadic and unconnected to the military efforts of the Allies. However the French Resistance soon became much better organized and coordinated with Britain.

The problem of the Resistance

The French Resistance became a huge thorn in the German side. They cut communication lines, blew up railway tracks, derailed trains and felled trees to block road movements. They also increased their attacks on German soldiers.

In return, the Germans took French hostages from the general population and authorized increasingly violent reprisals. In February 1944 General Field Marshal Hugo Sperrle issued orders stating that if any members of the French Resistance forces attacked the German Army, immediate and severe countermeasures should be taken. The Germans considered Vichy France as part of the Reich, and viewed

OVERLEAF: The quiet, unsophisticated way of life in a small rural French village between the wars is shown by this image of Oradour taken between 1920 and 1930.

the partisans as terrorists. During the whole term of the German occupation an estimated 30,000 French civilian hostages were shot in order to intimidate others.

The surprise in Normandy

The Germans got the biggest shock imaginable on 6 June 1944. Their 'thousand-year Reich' was suddenly under attack from the greatest invasion force the world had ever seen: 150,000 men in a flotilla of 5,000 vessels had landed on the beaches of northern France. D-Day.

Hitler dithered, and the invading Allies got a foothold in occupied France. Finally, he responded and ordered support troops to move north. One of these units was the 2nd SS-Panzer Division, under command of *Sturmbannführer* Adolf Diekmann. These were highly disciplined, experienced soldiers who had previously seen three years of hard combat in the east.

On 7 June the Division set off from Montaubin on the 640 km (400 miles) journey north to help their overrun countrymen. Their progress was immediately hampered by roadblocks of felled trees and deadly skirmishes with the Resistance.

News also filtered through to them that Resistance fighters had abducted Diekmann's colleague, *Sturmbannführer* Helmut Kämpfe. The capture of Kämpfe seems to have been the last straw for Diekmann. In the afternoon he ordered his SS troops in to the village of Oradour-sur-Glane.

In the early afternoon around 200 troops from the 2nd SS-Panzer Division began scouring the isolated farms and houses south of Oradour-sur-Glane. Everyone they found – male, female, young, old, sick – was herded towards the town. The soldiers torched the buildings as they left.

In town, most citizens were enjoying a leisurely Saturday lunch. Even when several trucks full of troops drove in they weren't alarmed. Nothing much ever happened in the village and hardly any Germans had even been in it before. The locals had no particular reason to fear anything.

The massacre

Sturmbannführer Diekmann used an interpreter to order that all citizens assemble in the market place for an identity check. This news was disseminated by the village crier, also the village smith, who broadcast it round the streets to the beat of his drum. Virtually all villagers heeded the call and gathered in the square; only a handful became suspicious and made a break for it over the fields.

The people gathered in a calm and orderly fashion; they knew they hadn't done anything wrong so they weren't scared. This peace soon dissipated though – once assembled, their papers weren't checked. Diekmann instead announced that his men would search for a cache of guns and ammunition, which he had heard was hidden in the town.

The men of the village were taken to barns and garages. Machine guns had already been set up in readiness in these locations.

The women and children were marched up the main street and driven into the local church. As they clustered together in terror they heard gunfire. It was the men of the town being shot.

The men were shot in the legs. Straw and firewood were packed around the survivors and they were burned to death. At least 190 men were killed in the barns.

The Germans then set the church ablaze with hand grenades, suffocating and burning those inside. Any woman or child seen escaping the flames was shot. A total of 247 women and 205 children died at the church. An unfortunate group of six cyclists, on a day's tour from Limoges, were also rounded up. They were all shot.

After the killings, the soldiers looted and burned every home and shop in the village. They left for Normandy within days.

Five men survived the massacre by playing dead under the piled corpses of their friends. One woman escaped the church, by climbing through the sacristy window. She was shot as she fell, but managed to scramble into a garden and hide.

Aftermath

Diekmann's actions repelled even his own superiors. His commanding officer was 'shocked by this report and shaken to the core', and the man in overall charge of the German Army in the west, *Generalfeldmarschall* Erwin Rommel, immediately demanded an investigation. However, Diekmann was killed in battle in Normandy three weeks later. Helmut Kampfe was killed by the Resistance.

Standing trial

There was a military tribunal in Bordeaux in 1953, which tried the surviving German soldiers – sixty-five of the 200 involved. Some of the others were now in Russian-controlled East Germany, and would not be extradited. Another 14 were Alsatian by birth and were thus French nationals, although of German extraction. They claimed they had been forcefully drafted into the *Waffen*-SS against their will.

Many of the men on trial claimed that Sperrle's orders from February 1944 justified their actions. At the end of the tribunal twenty were found guilty to varying degrees. All were released from prison within five years.

The crumbling memorial

In 1945 the President of France, Charles de Gaulle, ordered that Oradour should remain untouched as a ruined reminder of the atrocity that had happened here. His wishes have been followed ever since, with the village being maintained as it was when the sun set on 10 June 1944. The only addition has been a museum. A new, replacement village was built nearby.

The blackened husks of 328 buildings stand just as they did when the fires cooled on the morning of 11 June 1944. The old tramline to Limoges still winds along the main street, but no tram will ever visit here again. The mayor's car is rusting in the road where he parked it on that very morning in 1944.

Everywhere are reminders of ordinary lives brutally cut short: a sewing machine in an alcove; signs on the walls for the baker, dentist, and doctor; a bicycle left by a doomed day-tripper. The walls of the church and the First World War memorial are pocked with bullet holes. The grassy nave is eerily silent.

Signs on the walls encourage the town's visitors to 'Souviens-toi': *Remember*. Such words are unnecessary. Once seen, Oradour-sur-Glane is impossible to forget.

GIERSDORF CHURCH

POLAND
Giersdorf Church

DATE ABANDONED	TYPE OF PLACE	LOCATION	REASON	INHABITANTS	CURRENT STATUS
c. 1945	Church	Poland	War	0	Abandoned

THOUSANDS OF CHURCHES FELL VICTIM TO THE SECOND WORLD WAR, BROUGHT DOWN BY BOMBS, FIRE OR TANKS. A FEW, SUCH AS THIS TINY CHAPEL, LAY IN DISPUTED TERRITORY AND WERE SIMPLY FORGOTTEN WHEN THE LOCAL FAITHFUL LEFT.

Hallowed be thy name

Even in decay this tiny Protestant church is exquisite. The unusual oval-shaped building is three storeys tall with a small tower on top. Completed in 1797, it lies 100 km (62 miles) from Wrocław, in the town of Żeliszów, Poland, and has not seen a Sunday service in 70 years.

Before 1945, the town of Żeliszów lay within Germany and was known as Giersdorf. At the end of the Second World War, almost all Germans were forced to leave this area and the church lost its congregation. It hasn't been worshipped in since, like nearly all German-built churches in Poland. Żeliszów has another church that is active today.

The floors in the upper levels have now gone, leaving just the thick wooden beams. The roof has been pierced in many places, opening the body of the church up to everything the heavens can throw at it. The pews have gone, as have most of the trappings of religious worship. However, chiselled into the stone of two arches is a pair of quotations, their gothic script putting the nearby graffiti to shame. On the left is a verse from 1 Timothy, which translates as: *'That is a true and a precious word, that Jesus Christ came into the world, to bless the sinners.'* On the right the inscription reads: *'Come here to me, all you who are miserable and laden, I want to refresh you.'* It is from Matthew 11: 28.

A more famous brother

Lost and lonely though it is, this church was designed by Carl Langhans, the architect of the famous Brandenburg Gate in Berlin. This monumental arch was commissioned as a symbol of peace by the Prussian King Frederick William II in 1788, and is one of Germany's best-known landmarks.

The Gate was badly damaged by Allied bombs in the Second World War and was fenced off during the Cold War. In 2002 it was fully restored and now stands triumphantly at the heart of the bold new Berlin. Meanwhile, its cousin, the chapel, Langhans' tiny little masterpiece, is lying forgotten and rotting in a lost corner of the former German Empire.

TOP RIGHT: The oval church has two tiered galleries.

BOTTOM RIGHT: Biblical texts and graffiti adorn the walls.

OVERLEAF: The wood on the first floor is rotting, but still beautiful.

GRAUN

Graun

ITALY

DATE ABANDONED	TYPE OF PLACE	LOCATION	REASON	INHABITANTS	CURRENT STATUS
1950	Village	Italy	Hydroelectric scheme	2,200	Submerged

FOR 600 YEARS THE BELL TOWER WAS AT THE CENTRE OF DAILY LIFE IN THIS REMOTE ALPINE VILLAGE. THEN IT WAS DROWNED, ALONG WITH THE VILLAGE IT SERVED, TO DELIVER POWER TO HOMES FAR AWAY. TODAY IT POKES JUST ABOVE THE RESERVOIR'S SURFACE, A SYMBOL OF HOPE AND ENDURANCE – BUT ITS BELLS WILL NEVER RING AGAIN.

The church tower's walls have been reinforced to help them resist the crushing force of winter ice.

No man is an island

The locals say that on a clear winter's day the bells can still be heard echoing across the frozen lake, but they were actually removed from the fourteenth century church of Graun (known as *Curon Venosta* in Italian) before the village was flooded. However, looking out at the lonely bell tower, water stretching out all around it to the mountains on the horizon, it's as if some fearsome natural cataclysm has suddenly submerged the town. Such fantastic views make the legend easy to believe.

This is Lake Reschensee, which nestles near the borders with Austria and Switzerland in the southern Tyrol. The area is blessed with steep valleys and generous amounts of precipitation – making it perfect for locating hydroelectric schemes. In 1950 this river valley was selected as an ideal water storage site, and the villages of Graun, St. Valentin and Reschen were evacuated.

Even if one were to scuba dive beneath the lake's surface there isn't much else of old Graun to see. The church was deconsecrated and its graves relocated from the churchyard to a new resting place overlooking the drowned town. The body of the church was then demolished leaving only its bell tower intact.

A replacement village, also called Graun, was built higher up on the hillside above the new waterline. Today the half-submerged bell tower is a famous landmark, and forms the centrepiece of the commune's coat of arms.

The lake is popular with water sports enthusiasts who often splash past the belfry. In the deep frosts of winter it can be possible to walk out to the church tower across the ice. The tower has been strengthened, to help prevent water freezing in gaps in the masonry and thus causing the structure to crack.

Graun is perhaps the best-known flooded church, but it is far from being the only one. It seems that while we are happy to sacrifice houses for a new source of water power, we find it harder to completely destroy a holy building, no matter where we come from.

WAIUTA

DATE ABANDONED	TYPE OF PLACE	LOCATION	REASON	INHABITANTS	CURRENT STATUS
1951	Gold mining town	South Island, New Zealand	Economic	601	Partly preserved

WAIUTA WAS A PROSPECTOR'S DREAM: A BONANZA MADE GOOD IN THE GOLD FRENZY THAT SEIZED NEW ZEALAND'S SOUTH ISLAND. FOR NEARLY HALF A CENTURY IT GREW, BLOOMED, AND THEN, AS SUDDENLY AS IT HAD WINKED INTO EXISTENCE, THE TOWN'S GOLDEN LIGHTS WENT OUT FOREVER.

Gold in the wilderness

The coloured clapboard schoolhouse, barber's shop, cottages and russet-red chimneys stand as a small but noble outpost of civilization in the wilds of New Zealand's South Island. There is a tumbling stream, forests and views of the far Southern Alps, which are crowned with snow in the winter. Mighty Mount Cook can be glimpsed on a clear day. Tourists understandably stop by to have a picnic, snap some pictures and learn a little history in a pleasant few hours. However, when Waiuta was actually inhabited it was a hard, stony and dirty place to live.

There had been several gold rushes in the South Island from the 1850s onwards, first in Otago, then on the West Coast. It was the prospect of striking it rich that first brought Europeans to many previously unexplored parts of the country.

A party of prospectors struck lucky by the Blackwater River in 1905, scrabbling some yellow metal from a shallow pit on King Edward VII's birthday; the lode of ore was known as the Birthday Reef thereafter. The find was sold on and a company formed to work it. By 1908 they had completed a mineshaft that plummeted 563 m (1,847 ft) into the earth's crust: the Blackwater Shaft.

At this depth was a 'reef' of quartz with a very precious impurity in the form of gold. Miners drilled, dug and blasted the quartz out of the reef and the rubble was winched to the surface for processing.

Life at the quartz face

The miners faced considerable dangers – a fall down the mineshaft was the most feared accident, but the job also took its toll in more subtle ways. To extract gold from quartz the ore must first be smashed into small pieces. This was either done by a battery of heavy iron stamps that pounded the rock, or by iron balls placed in revolving steel drums. Either way the air would be cloudy with drifting quartz dust, which caused the lethal lung condition of 'miner's phthisis' (now known as silicosis). Production also involved the use of poisonous chemicals, including cyanide, to wash the smallest particles of gold out. Not only the miners, but the townspeople in general were exposed to these dangers simply by living near to the works.

Waiuta drew fortune hunters from the North Island, Australia and as far afield as Europe. The mining company even brought forty specialist miners and their families all the way from Cornwall – these immigrants were known as 'Cousin Jacks'.

A second shaft was sunk even deeper in 1936, to 879 m (2,884 ft). This was the deepest hole in New Zealand, and when men stepped out of the cage at the bottom they were 300 m (984 ft) below the level of the distant sea.

Production increased and what had been a mining camp grew into a proper town. The company built a miners' hall, a school and a cottage hospital. The land around Waiuta is mostly steep and rocky, so the tailings, or waste rock, from the mine were piled up to form areas of flat land. A bowling green, tennis courts and a rugby pitch were built on these expanses. The town even had a swimming pool in its later days.

By 1936 a burgeoning community of 601 souls called this place home – this would be the high point in Waiuta's existence.

The Second World War halved the number of miners at work here. By the end of the war the mine was running at only one third of its previous output, and working here was no longer such an attractive prospect.

Trouble underground

On 9 July 1951 the Blackwater Shaft collapsed and water began pouring into the pit. The flooding was severe – too extensive to remedy when judged against the amount of gold that the lode still had to offer. The mine was closed. It had produced 21 tonnes (750,000 ounces) of gold from 1.3 million tonnes (1.5 million tons) of mined quartz – a rate of return of 0.002 per cent. There were no other viable forms of employment in Waiuta, and the residents began to move away.

Most of the buildings were dismantled for salvageable materials, but after a few months even that became a profitless activity and Waiuta's fate as a ghost town was sealed.

Waiuta today

This is still a remote place: the nearest sizable town is Greymouth, 58 km (36 miles) to the south, which only has a population of 10,000. Wiauta is 17 km (11 miles) up a winding dirt track from the quiet Grey Valley. It seems like a wonder that the prospectors ever found this place at all.

The old winding buildings have gone, but there are still plenty of abandoned structures here that tell the story of Waiuta. In the foundations of the old winding machine hall is the black maw of the main shaft itself, happily covered by a grill – it's a fearsome prospect to imagine descending nearly a kilometre into this cavern of hell in a small cage every day.

Scattered around the remains of the mine buildings are the barber's shop, the tumbledown shells of cottages and shops, the police station and the rugby field. One structure that appears to be a small potting shed was actually where a miner slept, ate and raised his family. Standing on its own is a complex piece of winding gear stamped with the name of its maker in Glasgow: this was state-of the-art when shipped here, now it has been reduced to a rusted lump of iron.

Compared with the forested hulks of the mountains, the buildings with their corroding corrugated iron roofs seem flimsy and ephemeral. This perhaps is the truth: for a few decades this place was highly valued for the metal in its mud. Now it is prized far less, but with beauty all around and an interesting story to tell, it may yet be valued in a different way.

KOLMANSKOP

NAMIBIA

○ Kolmanskop

DATE ABANDONED	TYPE OF PLACE	LOCATION	REASON	INHABITANTS	CURRENT STATUS
1956	Mining town	Namibia	Economic	1,140	Abandoned

IT WAS A FORTUNE HUNTER'S DREAM – A PLACE WHERE DIAMONDS LAY SHINING ON THE OPEN SAND. BUT THIS WEALTH WAS GUARDED BY AN ANCIENT, HOSTILE DESERT AND NOW AN OCEAN OF DUNES IS RECLAIMING THE TOWN FOR ITS OWN.

The city born of sand

Houses stand thigh-deep in sand, their doors forever stuck open. The wind blows sand in and sweeps it into shapely piles in the corners and corridors; it rarely blows it out again. The wooden rooms that once echoed to the hubbub of family life are now deadened into silence. Inch by creeping inch, Kolmanskop is being slowly swallowed by the restless sands of the Namib Desert. That the town should die by the desert's hand is only fitting, for it was from the desert that it was born, a little over a century ago.

What is now Namibia was Imperial Germany's first colony, founded in 1884 as German South-West Africa (Deutsch-Südwestafrika). It was established by a fortune-hunting merchant

called Adolf Lüderitz who bought land in the area from local chiefs. The coastal town of Lüderitz was named after him, but he struggled to turn his vast claim into a profit.

Britain and other colonizing powers had not even bothered to stake a claim to what was a brutally unforgiving landscape. The Namib has been a sandy wasteland for 55–80 million years, making it probably the oldest desert in the world. For hundreds of miles, a bleak coastline is backed by impenetrable sand seas.

Colossal dunes, among the largest in the world, reach over 300 m (980 ft) high and stretch for 32 km (20 miles). Capricious winds push them this way and that, and the dunes eventually erase all that stands in their way. Portuguese sailors called Namibia's coast 'The Gates of Hell' and even on today's maps it is marked as the Skeleton Coast – more than a thousand wrecked ships litter its sun-bleached strands.

Diamonds in the desert
For twenty years the colony struggled to grow although houses, roads, a railway and other infrastructure were built. Then, in 1908, a worker shifting sand off the railway tracks in Kolmanskop, a few kilometres from the coast, spotted a bright stone on his shovel. When this was confirmed to be a diamond, the area became the focus of a frenzy. Treasure hunters swarmed to the town in their hundreds,

eager to stumble upon the riches that stories said littered this desert.

No sooner had the treasure hunters gathered than the authorities created a *Sperrgebiet* (forbidden area), marking a vast diamond-rich area as out of bounds (it remains off limits to those without a permit even today). This no-go zone covers a strip of coastal land 320 km (200 miles) long and extending up to 100 km (62 miles) inland, covering 26,000 km², or 10,400 square miles – about 3 per cent of Namibia's total area.

Home far from home
Amid this bleak desert, the licensed diamond hunters built Kolmanskop (Afrikaans for 'Coleman's Hill') as a German town. That was what these expats knew how to build; it also reminded them of home in this alien place. They constructed fine German-style houses and a startling array of social facilities: a power station, school, ice factory and a hospital with the first x-ray equipment in the southern hemisphere. The gem hunters created plenty of things to occupy themselves with when they weren't digging: a theatre, sports hall, ballroom, skittle alley, casino and – incredibly, given its location – a swimming pool.

The early diamond miners made a lot of money, and the town could afford to expand in style. There was a street of shops including a butcher, baker and furniture maker.

The town had its own station, from where trains ran to the port town of Lüderitz. In the town's heyday just before the First World War, there were 300 German adults, 40 children and 800 native workers of the Owambo people. They had sifted over 900 kg (2,000 lb) of rough diamonds from the bleak sands.

As the major link between Kolmanskop and the outside world, the port of Lüderitz temporarily became Africa's richest town. However, this boom was not to last.

The conflict and the diamonds
The First World War brought a crash in the price of diamonds and new imperial masters for Kolmanskop. Neighbouring South Africa took advantage when German military forces were distracted elsewhere, and they seized the colonial reins. It ruled the territory from 1919 until 1990, when the nation of Namibia became independent.

Kolmanskop limped on as a diamond town after the First World War, but its field was nearly worked out. Viable gems became more costly to extract, and any dreams of getting rich quick evaporated. The town began to decline.

Then in the late 1920s, even richer alluvial diamond deposits were discovered 240 km (150 miles) further south near Oranjemund. As quickly as they had arrived, the fortune hunters left for deserts new. Kolmanskop's star had burned fast and bright: it was born, grew up and died all within forty years. The very last inhabitants left in 1956. The town was deserted, and left to the desert.

The sands of time
Kolmanskop has not yet been completely engulfed, and the photogenic ruins have proved popular with the plucky tourists who make it to this lost corner of the world. In 1980, when this area was still administered by South Africa, the diamond conglomerate De Beers established a museum here and restored several buildings.

The glory days when diamonds could be picked by hand from the sand are hard to imagine now. Half a century of punishing winds has nearly demolished most of the elegant villas. Many others are being infiltrated by the dunes. Room after room is flooded by golden waves, contoured in shimmering peaks and troughs.

The encroaching desert is a constant, poignant reminder that while a diamond may be forever, a diamond town certainly is not.

DETROIT

Detroit

UNITED STATES OF AMERICA

DATE ABANDONED	TYPE OF PLACE	LOCATION	REASON	INHABITANTS	CURRENT STATUS
1950s onwards	Industrial city	Michigan, USA	Economic	1.8 million down to 700,000	Dereliction throughout the city

DETROIT WAS ONCE AMERICA'S FOURTH BIGGEST CITY AND THE WORLD'S MOTOR-MANUFACTURING CAPITAL. THIS INDUSTRIAL BEHEMOTH WAS FAMED FOR THE ARCHITECTURE BOUGHT BY ITS WEALTH – BUT NOW THE CARMAKERS AND THEIR WORKERS HAVE MOSTLY GONE, AND WHOLE NEIGHBOURHOODS HAVE BEEN LEFT TO ROT.

An abandoned factory stands near General Motors' world headquarters.

The rusting of motor city
In July 2013 the city of Detroit filed the largest municipal bankruptcy debt in US history, at $18.5 billion. Images of abandoned Detroit hit the newspapers worldwide, but the city's problems hadn't just stemmed from the 2008 financial crash, or even from a recent drop in sales of American-built cars; Detroit had been in decline for half a century.

Detroit gets into gear...

The 'Paris of the West' was its nickname in the late nineteenth century, and while this may have been overselling it a little, Detroit certainly had an array of fabulous architecture to rival even the world's leading cities. Wealthy shipping magnates built grand houses, and wide European-style boulevards created a modern and ambitious metropolis.

Ideally sited at a nexus of trade routes around the Great Lakes, Detroit developed into a major transport centre. There was a significant shipbuilding industry and the booming construction and manufacturing drew thousands upon thousands of European immigrants. Henry Ford built his first car here in 1896, and there were soon dozens of factories making cars and parts, earning Detroit its epithet of 'Motor City'. Ford, Chrysler and General Motors became the world's 'Big Three' car makers, all based in Detroit. General Motors sold more vehicles than any other manufacturer on the planet for seventy-seven consecutive years from 1931 to 2007.

The city grew out – and up – on the flood of wealth. Striking Art Deco skyscrapers rose ever higher and by 1920 Detroit was the United States' fourth largest city. It retained that status for exactly thirty years, and then its star began to fade.

...and goes in reverse

No sooner had the auto industry reached its greatest heights, than its fortunes were already tumbling. In the 1950s several giant firms merged, which boosted the bottom line of many companies but left huge manufacturing plants derelict. Packard and Hudson were among the once-proud marques to vanish. Their huge plants were decommissioned and became some of the largest abandoned industrial sites on earth.

The industry became the epitome of an oligopoly. Manufacturers had such a rich home market that innovation stagnated. Overseas manufacturers, meanwhile, were much more nimble and forward-focused.

Veterans returning from the Second World War received incentives to buy new homes thanks to the GI Bill, which in turn encouraged developers to create new suburbs. These were linked by a newly built network of highways and freeways. The idea of the densely populated city centre passed into American history, and low-density housing where the car was the main mode of transport became the trend. A spacious house in the suburbs and an easy commute in a big American car was the post-war reality for millions of ordinary people.

The 1970s hit the town particularly hard. The oil crises in 1973 and 1979 pushed fuel prices up and suddenly

economy trumped patriotism in car-buyers' minds. More and more foreign cars hit the American market and home output fell. The city saw particularly bad race riots and a growth in drug-fuelled crime. Unemployment rose as its core industries collapsed.

The city of Detroit had 1.8 million citizens in 1950. In 2010, just 713,777 people called it home, a drop of more than 60 per cent. The population fell 25 per cent between 2000 and 2010, with whole districts hollowed out. It is now America's 18th-largest city.

Detroit's rotting core

The result of this population exodus is urban decay on an epic scale. There are at least 40,000 vacant homes, apartments and commercial buildings throughout the city.

Habitation is so sparse in some areas that the city struggles to deliver emergency services, refuse disposal and other services to the few isolated residents. The authorities are gently encouraging them to move into more populated locations. For many derelict areas the only feasible solution has been to demolish great swathes of buildings and remove street lighting, thus returning unused quarters to the wilds. Or rather, to leave them to the 20,000 stray dogs that now roam this waste-world in packs.

The Packard plant was once the most modern car-making facility in the world.

In 2011, the owners of over half of Detroit's 305,000 properties couldn't pay their tax bills. Their empty pockets meant the city coffers were critically underfunded. There were seventy-seven city blocks with only one owner who paid taxes.

This means that Detroit has perhaps the greatest variety of abandoned buildings anywhere on earth. There are derelict shops, churches, synagogues, railway stations, theatres, nursing centres and block upon block upon block of housing.

Michigan Central Station

Michigan Central Station was Detroit's main rail terminal and a masterpiece of the Beaux-Arts classical style. Designed by the same team who created the magnificent Grand Central Terminal in New York City, it was the tallest railway building in the world when completed, its 18-storey tower reaching 70 m (230 ft). The marble walls and vaulted stucco ceilings of the main waiting room were designed to echo the serene majesty of an ancient Roman bathhouse. In the central ticket hall were Doric columns and an elegant shopping arcade. The concourse had a fine skylight of hammered copper.

Passengers arriving by streetcar entered the station's arcade, which was lined with retail venues including a cigar store, pharmacy and newsstand, as well as an information booth, parcel drop-off and telephone booths. Thirteen large and airy floors of offices were stacked above the concourse.

It opened in 1913, when the nascent car-building industry had not yet conquered American transportation. The station was the crossroads for railway tracks entering Detroit, and soon 200 trains a day steamed out of it. Queues of passengers stretched right through the building's beautiful halls. However, the station was deliberately sited outside the city's centre as a hub to attract surrounding development, and that never materialized as planned. Passengers arrived there by streetcar, which became a problem when the streetcars stopped running in the 1930s. After the Second World War, passenger numbers steadily dwindled. Despite a renovation in the 1970s, the station finally closed in 1988, replaced by a new station several miles away. Decay took over in earnest.

The building enjoyed some repair work in 2012, but its owner faces a major challenge. The basement, which contains boilers and heating pipes, is largely flooded. The hundreds of smashed windows have let two decades of Detroit weather do their worst to the inside. Restoring the whole building would cost a fortune. Demolishing it is probably out of the question though – it was added to the National Register of Historic Places in 1975. So it remains in limbo: the odd bit of repair work here, some broken windows replaced there, but mostly it is rotting by the hour.

The Michigan Building

'It is not merely a theater for Detroit. It is a theater for the whole world. It is designed to be the greatest showplace of the Middle West.'

So said John H. Kunsky, owner of the Michigan Theater, shortly after its opening in 1926. He had reason to speak in such grandiose terms: his theatre was magnificent. In its heyday the Marx Brothers, Betty Grable and Bob Hope trod its boards and entertained 4,050 people at a time.

It was still hosting rock bands in the early 1970s, but finally closed in 1976. The tenants of the offices upstairs threatened to leave unless parking was provided for them. So the building's owners stripped out the stage, seating and dressing rooms and installed a parking structure. The decorated ceilings of the auditorium and the remains of the stage arch now hang in space above the oil-slicked concrete of the ninth floor of the parking garage.

Detroit's future

The city is restructuring its debts and there has been some reinvestment in the downtown area. Some young professionals have moved in downtown, but the automotive industry will never return to its peak of the 1950s. There is also still a problem with violent crime in many areas. The grassed-over neighbourhoods are so vast that it's unlikely they will see much human life return.

The city may be slowly rusting, but its long decline has allowed some of its glories to be preserved. As other American cities grew in the 1960s and 1970s, they tore down and rebuilt many of their finest buildings from earlier in the century. In Detroit there was no profit in either rebuilding or demolishing them, and so they remain as skeletons – the bones of a city's full-blooded dream.

ABOVE LEFT: Nature flourishes in an abandoned church.
BELOW LEFT: Michigan Central Station.

LION CITY

DATE ABANDONED	TYPE OF PLACE	LOCATION	REASON	INHABITANTS	CURRENT STATUS
1959	Town	Zhejiang Province, China	Building a power station	295,000	Submerged

THE 'ATLANTIS OF THE EAST' IS A 1,700-YEAR-OLD CHINESE TOWN DROWNED BY THE WATERS OF A MAN-MADE LAKE. DESPITE ITS FATE THE TOWN'S BUILDINGS ARE REMARKABLY WELL-PRESERVED, PRESENTING A UNIQUE TIME CAPSULE OF A FORGOTTEN AGE.

The city that was sacrificed

Over a thousand emerald islands speckle the surface of Qiandao Lake, but even more beautiful is what lies below the ripples – an ancient city that stands intact under 40 m (130 ft) of water.

Shi Cheng earned its name ('Lion City') because it sits at the foot of Wu Shi ('Five Lion') Mountain. The city was founded during the Dong Han dynasty (AD 25–200) and it soon prospered, becoming the political and economic hub of Zhejiang province. The bustling life of a country town continued untroubled for the next 1,750 years.

Then in 1959 the Chinese Government drew up plans for the Xin'anjiang Hydropower Station, the country's first large-scale power plant. This would require what was then the biggest dam in China, a 105 m (344 ft) tall and 466.5 m (1,531 ft) long monster. The power station would deliver 845 megawatts of power to the growing city of Shanghai; the damming of the Xin'an River would create a lake the size of Singapore.

While this was good news for Shanghai's citizens, it was bad news for residents of Lion City, which would be completely submerged by the new reservoir. Over a quarter of a million people were relocated. They took their belongings with them, but the structures in the city itself were simply left. Then the sluice gates were closed, the river began backing up into a 100 km (60 mile) long lake, and inch by inch the ancient metropolis was flooded. The mountain that had towered over the town for nearly two millennia was itself overcome by water.

Sleeping in the deep

For half a century Lion City slumbered in its watery tomb, forgotten about by all except its displaced residents. Then, around 2002, some curious geographers began to wonder if it still existed. After much research they eventually located the drowned town using sonar equipment.

Shi Cheng was rediscovered by divers in 2008 – and what a treasure chest they found. The first surprise was that the huge circular city wall, which enclosed an area equal to sixty-two football pitches, was completely intact. Within this lay a labyrinth of temples, arches, staircases, houses and roadways, much of which was still in pristine condition, despite its fifty-year drowning. Delicate carvings could still be seen and even wooden pillars, stairs and balustrades were in surprisingly good condition.

The city has since been visited by many more curious divers and is being promoted as a must-see site for adventurous tourists.

HUMBERSTONE & SANTA LAURA

Humberstone

CHILE

DATE ABANDONED	TYPE OF PLACE	LOCATION	REASON	INHABITANTS	CURRENT STATUS
1960	200 mining communities	Chile	Economic	3,700	UNESCO World Heritage Site

THE WORLD'S LARGEST SALTPETRE DEPOSITS SUPPORTED 200 THRIVING MINING COMMUNITIES AND PRODUCED GREAT PROSPERITY FOR CHILE. THE PROFITS LOOKED ENDLESS – UNTIL A SYNTHETIC ALTERNATIVE RENDERED THE RESOURCE WORTHLESS. THE TOWNS, AND THE WEALTH THEY WERE BUILT ON, WERE LEFT TO THE DESERT.

Land of white gold

It would take something special to lure thousands of ordinary people into a life in the driest non-polar desert on earth. The Atacama Desert's average rainfall is about 15 mm (0.59 inches) per year, although the coastal town of Iquique receives only 1–3 mm (0.04–0.12 inches) and at several weather stations it has never rained at all. It is a very, very hard place to live. Yet it did indeed have something worth getting thirsty for: sodium nitrate.

Sodium nitrate, also known as Chilean saltpetre, was an ingredient in gunpowder. This made it valuable, particularly so during the European arms race that preceded the First World War. Saltpetre was also an ingredient in fertilizer, which created an even bigger demand as cereal production spread to unexploited lands in the USA, Argentina and Russia. Chilean saltpetre was used on the burgeoning coffee plantations in Brazil, and sugar plantations in Cuba and the Dominican Republic.

Northern Chile was blessed with the world's greatest natural deposits of saltpetre, held in a mineral ore called caliche. It was so valuable that Chile fought the 'Saltpetre War' against Peru and Bolivia in 1879 for control of the best resources.

As the huge deposits began to be extracted, towns housing thousands of workers sprang up in the *pampas* (plains) of the Atacama Desert. The inhabitants, or *pampinos*, defied their brutal environment to work and raise families for several generations.

One of the largest settlements was Humberstone, sited 48 km (30 miles) to the east of Iquique. This was named after an English chemical engineer, James Humberstone, who founded works here in 1862 and whose later innovations made the extraction process even more profitable. (Most of the saltpetre production facilities in Chile were owned by British interests.)

TOP RIGHT: The main processing facility at Santa Laura. This was smaller and less successful than the one in Humberstone.

BOTTOM RIGHT: A classroom in the primary school, which was built in 1894 and expanded in 1936.

OVERLEAF TOP: A rusting pumphouse.

OVERLEAF BOTTOM: The swimming pool was built in 1936 using iron salvaged from a shipwreck.

Humberstone became the hub of a vast saltpetre production centre. Deposits had first been taken out of the area by mule, which limited production. With the arrival of the railways in the second half of the nineteenth century however, the growth of the mines was rapid. There were over 200 works in the region, interconnected with railways that also ran to the ports in the west. By 1905 there were 1,800 km (1,120 miles) of track crisscrossing northern Chile, and by 1913 this had risen to a remarkable 5,000 km (3,000 miles). In 1912 there were 45,000 workers in northern Chile's saltpetre mines.

A smaller mining plant, Santa Laura, was founded in 1872 just 1.5 km (0.9 miles) from Humberstone. Even this had swollen to a town of 450 families during the booming 1920s.

With vast deposits still waiting in the earth to be exploited, it seemed that Humberstone's glory days would go on indefinitely. However, inventors in Europe were about to inadvertently kill these towns overnight and forever.

Synthetic nitrates
At the beginning of the twentieth century, the German chemist Fritz Haber invented a way of producing ammonia from the atmosphere. His colleague Carl Bosch later developed Haber's process on an industrial scale. Both Haber and Bosch received the Nobel Prize for their work. After the war their process continued to be used by the European producers of fertilizers and pharmaceuticals, who found it much more convenient to obtain their nitrates closer to home. For the Chilean saltpetre mines it was a death sentence.

By the 1930s Humberstone was producing just 10 per cent of the saltpetre it had done ten years before. By the 1950s, output was down to 3 per cent. Santa Laura closed in 1958, Humberstone followed the next year. There was nothing else to stay in the Atacama for, so the workers left.

Chile's white-golden age was over.

The sites today
Machinery, rusted into spars and fragments, lies scattered around the blinding sands. Narrow-gauge locomotives, which once carried the white gold to the shining Pacific in the west, stand shattered.

In the houses there are pictures of family members still hanging on the walls. There are items of clothing, shoes and *fichas* (tokens used instead of cash) still lying where they were discarded over half a century ago.

Many of the buildings that remain in Humberstone date from the 1930s and 1940s, when a new owner invested in the mine in an attempt to ensure its survival. Day-to-day life would then have been of a reasonable quality for the 3,700 people who lived here. The town had its own theatre that showed Mexican films and Spanish *zarzuelas* (operettas). This building still stands – just – but inside its once-soft red velvet chairs are dusty and tattered. The town also had, in a triumph of desert engineering, its own swimming pool. This is now a rusting iron tank scrawled with chalk graffiti, its diving boards forever bereft of children showing off.

After the closure, the machinery was sold for scrap and would have been dismantled had the Chilean Government not declared Humberstone a national monument in 1970. The site was also named a UNESCO World Heritage Site in 2005. It's on the list of World Heritage Sites in danger – not only from the harsh desert conditions, but also from earthquakes and vandalism.

However, Humberstone still stands as the best-preserved of all the old saltpetre works, and its listing by UNESCO should ensure its survival. Every year it hosts 'Saltpetre Week', which gathers together people from all over the Pampa who have a connection to the site, including former saltpetre workers and their descendants.

Pinochet's prison camps
A few of the other saltpetre works found a gruesome new role after they were closed – as concentration camps. Pisagua, 190 km (118 miles) north of Iquique, is a very isolated port that nevertheless grew wealthy in the nineteenth century on the traffic of saltpetre. Like Humberstone it then declined in the twentieth century. When the dictatorship of General Pinochet needed somewhere to lose its political prisoners, it chose here. A prison camp was established, and many hundreds of detainees were delivered here to be tortured and killed. The once-flourishing Pisagua is today a true ghost town. Its 250 remaining residents scratch out a sombre life on the cusp of the desert and the ocean, harvesting algae and shellfish.

CHINGUETTI

DATE ABANDONED	TYPE OF PLACE	LOCATION	REASON	INHABITANTS	CURRENT STATUS
Twentieth century	Desert town	Mauritania	Environmental	20,000	Endangered

○Chinguetti
MAURITANIA

FACING DOWN THE SAHARAN SANDS IS A MEDIEVAL TRADING TOWN WITH A FASCINATING SECRET. HIDDEN AMONG ITS DESERTED MUD-BRICK HUTS IS A ONCE GREAT ANCIENT REALM OF SCHOLARSHIP AND WISDOM.

The cultural oasis

The lonely wind-blown track is almost lost in the belly of an interminable high-sided wadi. Over the lip of the crumbling clifftops are dune seas spreading flat out to the horizon. Not that travellers here usually see much on this road: most are on the go pre-dawn, before the remorseless West African sun has had a chance to gain its burning strength. Finally, many bumpy hours after they left the last twenty-first century town, the track jolts them back into the thirteenth century at Chinguetti.

Here are all the things one might expect from an ancient ghost town at the edge of the Sahara Desert. Dunes, scattered palms, the setting sun casting long shadows of men and camels on the ochre sand. The houses are built of reddish

The Friday Mosque in Chinguetti.

stone and mud bricks, with flat roofs set on timbers shaped from palm trunks. The most ancient dwellings have doors hand-carved from enormous acacia trees, which have not grown here for centuries. The featureless, desert-proof outer walls of many homes belie elegant courtyards and patios within.

The architectural gem of the old city is the Friday Mosque: a muezzin has called the faithful to prayer from its square minaret five times a day for over 700 years. Other notable buildings include an arched fortress once staffed by the French Foreign Legion and a tall water tower. This would be reward enough for the sweating, squinting travellers, but Chinguetti also has an astonishing secret that no other abandoned town can boast of: it is home to the world's most endangered library of rare books.

The Oxford of the desert

Chinguetti formed as a *ksar*, or fortified market town, at the hub of several spoke-like trade routes that threaded their way across the surrounding sands. Many pilgrims heading to

Mecca from the western Maghreb came here to meet their fellows and form into groups for the dangerous journey east to Arabia. For those too sick or old to reach Mecca, Chinguetti was a destination in itself.

In time, this meant that Chinguetti too became a sacred place. It also grew into a medieval centre of learning to rival Oxford, Cambridge and Paris: scholars from all over northern Africa came here to study science, medicine, religion, law, mathematics and astronomy. A bustling town of 20,000 people grew up to support them. Chinguetti became the seventh holy city of Islam and was known as the 'City of Libraries'.

Volumes of wisdom
The pages are gazelle skin, the covers goatskin. The writing ranges over science, literature and religion, and includes some of the most important Islamic texts. At least 6,000 volumes, many of them dating to the ninth century, sleep on shelves in these mud-brick buildings.

The books were kept in family-run libraries that were passed down from one generation to the next for centuries. When the desert forced a family to leave, they took their precious volumes with them. There are around ten libraries today; in the 1950s there were thirty.

If this were the Vatican vaults or British Library, these volumes would be held in climate-controlled rooms under lock and key. Here their only protection from the abrasive dust, sandstorms and occasional flash floods is a cardboard binder. Many books have survived several centuries of arid weather only to become a meal for rats.

The largest extant collection contains 1,600 books and is one of the oldest libraries in the Islamic world, with many important Qur'anic texts. Its books are housed in rusting iron boxes. The library is trying to look like a place of scholarship, with filing cabinets and reading desks, but it seems incongruous to the point of absurdity with the desert wind whipping sand in through the open door.

Protecting the books would take money and that is in short supply. Only a handful of scholars and the few western travellers who venture out to see the libraries put any money in the pockets of the nomadic guardians. The tragedy is that the very act of showing the books to visitors hastens their decay.

Nor will any funds be forthcoming from the government. Mauritania is about the size of Egypt, and three-quarters of its land is desert. This proportion has been increasing since the mid-1960s due to a series of extended, severe droughts. Today it is a poor country with many deeply rooted problems. It was not illegal to own slaves here until 2007, and it is estimated that up to 600,000 Mauritanians, or 20 per cent of the population, are still enslaved. Political turmoil has seen two coups since 2000. Building a new library is not high on any leader's list of priorities.

The ever-marching sands
The Sahara is ambitious and it never rests. In caves near to Chinguetti are Stone Age paintings of the area as a lush grassland: cows graze the grass; giraffes munch the treetops; people rest by the waterside. The desert is building an empire in the land where men from Western Europe once scrabbled to expand theirs. At Chinguetti's western edge, where once the town's beasts grazed at pasture, huge dunes now stand like invading soldiers, ready to march when the winds order them.

The dunes in some areas of the southern Sahara are expanding at a rate of 48 km (30 miles) per year. The increasing desertification of the area is why most of the people left, and why they will never come back. UNESCO has given Chinguetti World Heritage Site status, which accords it some legal protection, but the desert doesn't abide by human laws.

Most of Chinguetti's abandoned houses are roofless and exposed to the drifting sand. In the few sound structures, families live in varying states of residence. They care for the mosque, tend to the libraries and work to earn money from the scattered tourists who make it this far.

Chinguetti is a shadow of an ancient civilization cast into our modern world. It's likely that this remote town will be wholly swallowed by the Saharan sands within a lifetime, and its memory will fade entirely. Until then, it will remain a haunting, humbling place to visit.

Centuries-old volumes lie on the rudimentary shelves of Ahel Ahmed Wanane Library.

NORTH BROTHER ISLAND

North Brother Island
**UNITED STATES
OF AMERICA**

DATE ABANDONED	TYPE OF PLACE	LOCATION	REASON	INHABITANTS	CURRENT STATUS
1963	Quarantine island	New York City	Outdated	Around 100	Abandoned/Bird sanctuary

AN ISLAND JUST 350 METRES FROM THE BRONX WAS HOME TO LEPERS AND A MEDICAL ODDITY CARRYING A PLAGUE SO INFECTIOUS THAT SHE LEFT DISEASE AND DEATH IN HER WAKE. NOW IT IS A QUIET WOODED WORLD, AN OASIS FOR MIGRANT BIRDS, UNHEEDED BY THE GREAT METROPOLIS THAT SURROUNDS IT.

The theatre where patients once found entertainment.

A walk on the wild side

Vines pour forth from empty windows like green waterfalls. A strangely flat forest floor turns out on closer inspection to be a car park. Proud mansions have been humbled into crumbling shells by ivy. Pavements are split by trees. Hungry waves have devoured waterfront barriers and digested a road that once toured the coast. Welcome to North Brother Island, a remarkable example of a community abandoned by humans and utterly engulfed by nature in just a few decades. But what makes this place truly extraordinary is that it sits right in the heart of New York City.

Uninhabited North Brother Island lies in the East River between the Bronx and Queens: 1.4 million people on one side, 2.3 million on the other. Few people among those millions even know that North Brother Island exists. Yet, just a century ago, it was one of the most feared and famous locations in the city.

Quarantine island

No humans lived on North Brother Island until 1885. It was a 20-acre wooded home to birds and small mammals. However, its quiet isolation made it the perfect place to quarantine New York's victims of infectious diseases, and in 1885 the Riverside Hospital was built amid the trees. The hospital primarily treated smallpox victims, although it later also took in patients with scarlet fever, typhus and leprosy.

Many of the doctors lived in mansion-like houses on the island. Other medical staff

came over by ferry from 138th Street in the Bronx. Patients arrived this way, too, although most of them never made the return trip.

Banished to die alone

For two decades, North Brother Island's most famous inhabitant was Mary Mallon. Born in Ireland in 1869, she emigrated to the USA and worked as a cook in New York. Her skills were much appreciated and she worked for several wealthy families. The only problem was that everywhere Mary went, typhoid fever followed her. Family after family succumbed to the disease, with at least fifty-three people becoming infected and three dying in outbreaks centred around Mary.

When the authorities traced Mary she was found to be perfectly healthy. Newspapers made her infamous as 'Typhoid Mary' and she became the scary monster in a thousand fireside tales. She was eventually identified as the first ever typhoid carrier never to show symptoms of the disease. This was a breakthrough for medical science, but a prison sentence for Mary: she was held at North Brother from 1915 until her death in 1938. She always vehemently denied that she carried the disease.

A change for the better

In 1935, Stanley Walker, the editor of the New Yorker, described North Brother Island as:

'...a dismal spot. Sitting there, one may see, as the best view, the gas tanks on the Bronx shore. Now and then a ferryboat glides past. At night the dirty water of the East River laps against the rocks, making a messy, ghostly noise.'

More modern hospitals were being built in New York and new treatments were reducing the need for quarantine. In the late 1930s the patients began to be moved out of Riverside.

The island welcomed a new type of resident in the 1940s: war veterans and their families. It blossomed into a semi-rural sanctuary amid the sprawling metropolis. Quiet roads – bordered by lawns and shaded by trees – wound between a scattering of buildings. But it was an inconvenient place to live. The city could only be reached by an irregular and slow ferry, and by 1951 most veterans had moved out.

The island's last human inhabitants were people who had nowhere else to go: heroin addicts. Peaceful it may have been, but the rehabilitation centre was also impractical and expensive. The last doctors, nurses and patients left on a boat for the city in 1963. Given its unpleasant recent history, the island was an easy place for the city to forget about.

North Brother's next tenant, Mother Nature, was quick to move in and make herself at home. Aerial photographs from the 1950s show that the vegetation was limited to clipped lawns and shady trees. When photographer Christopher Payne 'rediscovered' the island in 2008 he found brick buildings embroiled in foliage of near-jungle density. Inside he met ghosts: dormitories with rude graffiti daubed by long-dead patients; shelves of books unread for half a century; an X-ray from the Tuberculosis Pavilion; a Bronx phone book from 1961.

A glimpse into the past – or future?

You could reach North Brother Island in just ten minutes by boat from the Bronx's Barretto Point Park – although you would be breaking the law if you did. Public landing is prohibited both on safety grounds and because the island is now a protected nature reserve. Only a few council officials, guests and photographers have explored it. They report a profoundly strange place, where one can stand isolated in a forest amid half-decayed buildings and scurrying, fluttering wildlife and then hear car horns from the Bronx and loudspeakers from the huge prison on nearby Rikers Island filtering through the leafy canopy.

The New York Parks Department cares for thirteen other 'abandoned' islands within the city and there are dozens of inhabited islands. North Brother Island is a fascinating reminder that New York is, in geographical reality, an archipelago – a fact that may be hard to appreciate when you're having a bite to eat in the wilds of Greenwich Village.

TOP LEFT: This mighty tome was a ledger for prescriptions.

BOTTOM LEFT: The buildings are all but lost in the trees.

CRACO

DATE ABANDONED	TYPE OF PLACE	LOCATION	REASON	INHABITANTS	CURRENT STATUS
1963	Town	Italy	Natural disasters	1,800	Abandoned

CRACO WAS ONCE A PINNACLE OF LIFE, LEARNING AND ARCHITECTURE – A MEDIEVAL UNIVERSITY TOWN IN A SUPERLATIVE HILLTOP LOCATION. BUT WHEN THE EARTH ON WHICH IT STOOD CRUMBLED, THE ANCIENT STREETS CRACKED. THE HOUSES SPLIT AND CENTURIES OF EVERYDAY LIFE CAME TO AN END.

The ruined crown

From a distance it is one of those impossibly picturesque medieval towns that crown the rural Italian landscape. On closer inspection, however, it's clear that there are no cafés full of gossip and laughter, no washing hanging from the iron railings of the upper storey windows, no children playing in the labyrinthine alleys. The near thousand-year-old settlement of Craco is desolate, dusty and crumbling into the valley below.

Crushed underfoot

'Mezzogiorno' – land of the midday sun – is how Italians describe the southern part of their country. This is a landscape of lonely villages, empty valleys and bare, rocky landscapes. Shepherds still drive their flocks over stony hills and black-clad women thread washing across narrow alleys. In summer the sun beats the countryside like a hammer on copper; in winter this land can be surprisingly cold.

Basilicata is a small and mountainous area in this sun-scorched land, just at the instep of southern Italy's 'boot'. Much of its countryside is a barren, eroded wasteland. The soil is

generally poor and the earth lacks mineral riches. In the past, landowners deliberately deforested much of the area to increase what little revenues the land was producing. This only served to strip the soil and increase the likelihood of landslides.

Craco is typical of the medieval hill towns in this region. Lying 32 km (20 miles) inland from the Gulf of Taranto, it perches on a 400 m (1,312 ft) cliff overlooking the Cavone River valley. Life has been hard here over the last few centuries. In the 1880s more than half of all children died in the area before the age of 15. Large numbers of people risked the long journey to the USA in the early twentieth century: 1,500 families emigrated from the Craco area between 1892 and 1922. Whatever the perils of the unknown New World, worse was to follow for those who stayed in the Old.

The enemy beneath

Craco's position was a strategic triumph in the Middle Ages. The town commanded a superlative view of the surrounding landscape and was almost untouchable by invaders from afar. However, its greatly elevated position was also its weakness; Craco would be undone from within by its own traitorous foundations.

The hilltop might have seemed like solid rock, but much of it was a stony aggregate laid down on clay. Ravine-like faults cut unseen into the bedrock, forming unstable fissures that lurked just beneath the surface and extended to depths of 50 m (164 ft).

The land turned on Craco in the mid-twentieth century. A series of earthquakes between 1959 and 1972 triggered severe landslides that rattled Craco into ruins. Geologists had warned of the possibility of such seismic activity as early as 1910, but nothing was done to protect the town from destruction. In truth, given the town's straitened economic circumstances and the expense of the huge preventative engineering works that would have been required, it is easy to see why that was the case. From 1963, Craco's remaining 1,800 residents began to be evacuated to safer areas of Basilicata.

A return may have been conceivable, in theory – but in 1972 the landslides were followed by a flood that damaged the town further. A particularly severe earthquake in 1980 ruled out any possible rebuilding or repopulation. Ever.

Exploring Craco today

The few people visiting now are tourists who come to be led round a prescribed path, wearing compulsory hard hats at all times. They are accompanied by the sheep that roam the steep hillside and broken roads.

The town's centre was built squarely upon the perfidious clay, and it has suffered the greatest damage. Whole sides of buildings are missing; scaffolding erected to hold up walls is itself tumbling into the valley. Yet less than 50 years ago, this piazza was teeming with life.

Craco's heartbreakingly scenic ruination has made it an understandable choice of location for movie directors. The town has featured in the films *Saving Grace*, *Nativity*, and the James Bond adventure *Quantum of Solace*. In *The Passion of The Christ*, Craco is where Judas was hanged.

Thick vegetation chokes every inch of the main road out of town, but the street still rings with clear echoes of the town's beauty in centuries past: winding cobbled alleys, tall arching doorways, tiled roofs, elegant staircases, imposing towers and regal balconies. This must be the most beautiful mess in Italy.

CHITTAGONG

BANGLADESH

DATE ABANDONED	TYPE OF PLACE	LOCATION	REASON	INHABITANTS	CURRENT STATUS
Twentieth century	Ship graveyards	Bangladesh	Economic	Various passengers and crew	Abandoned/ Being recycled

Chittagong

MODERN MEANS OF TRANSPORT HAVE REVOLUTIONIZED OUR LIVES. SHIPS, CARS, PLANES AND TRAINS TAKE US EVERYWHERE WE NEED TO GO, ALMOST WHENEVER WE WANT. BUT WHERE DO WE TAKE THEM WHEN WE NO LONGER NEED THEM?

Breakers on the beach

What happens when ships the size of towns are no longer wanted? They are abandoned on the beaches in the Bay of Bengal. Here the shallow continental shelf allows ships to be simply run aground on the muddy strand. Teams of ship breakers then go out to break them up for scrap.

Shipbreaking here began at Sitakunda, near Chittagong in Bangladesh, in 1964 with the scrapping of a ship that had become accidentally beached. The suitable physical environment and local pool of cheap labour led to rapid growth. There are now twenty ship-breaking yards on an 8 km (5 mile) stretch of coast. This is the largest ship-breaking centre in the world, although there are others nearly as big in India and Pakistan.

Shipbreaking in the developed world is more regulated and hence more expensive. So most of this dirty, dangerous work is done here, where there is plenty of cheap labour and very little concern for health or safety.

Beached and broken

After 25–30 years at sea most ships have taken a hefty battering. At this point the cost of repair, maintenance and insurance exceeds the cost of obtaining a new ship, and the vessel is scrapped.

In one way, this is the ultimate in recycling: some of the largest vessels ever built are sliced apart and turned into scrap that supplies 80 per cent of Bangladesh's steel. Chemicals,

Ships are broken up on the beach at Bhatiary Yard, Chittagong.

engineering equipment and any last pockets of oil and fuel can also be salvaged. Three million people are supported by the industry. The problems, however, are many.

The pollution is astonishing. Black oil turns the waves to sludge. Mud has been turned orange-red with rust. Hideous green slicks of chemicals pool in the sand at low tide. One or two ships arrive for breaking every week, so the environment never gets a chance to recover. This short stretch has to be one of the most despoiled coastlines on the planet. Incredibly, some fishermen still rig their nets amid the toxic debris.

Braving death for a few dollars a day
These ships were not designed to be broken up; on the contrary, they were built to withstand the pounding of the oceans. On average it will take fifty men working long hours six days a week around three months to reduce a medium-sized ship of 40,000 tonnes to scrap.

Safety is virtually non-existent: workers break the huge vessels up by hand wearing sandals and no protective clothing. When a chunk of ship has been sliced off it falls in a shower of steel splinters and hazardous debris. The piece will then be hauled up the beach by huge chains to be broken down further. Around 40 per cent of the labourers are children. Many of the ships contain toxic chemicals, asbestos, and heavy metals such as lead.

An average of fifteen workers are killed every year, and over fifty are badly injured. Many workers' arms and legs are criss-crossed with savage scars, known with bleak humour as 'Chittagong tattoos'. Other men have lost fingers or been blinded in one eye.

An average monthly wage for this grindingly hard and highly dangerous work is around US $300. About half of this will be spent on rent in the shanty-like shacks run by the yard's owners. Despite the danger and the low pay, around 25,000 people have come from all over Bangladesh to seek a livelihood here.

L'ÎLE-AUX-MARINS

DATE ABANDONED	TYPE OF PLACE	LOCATION	REASON	INHABITANTS	CURRENT STATUS
1965	Fishing community	Near Newfoundland, Canada	Hardship	c. 700	Occasional seasonal use

THESE WERE THE HOUSES, CHURCH AND SCHOOL OF PEOPLE WHO FISHED THE SEAS AT THE VERY EDGE OF THE ATLANTIC. THEIRS WAS A BRUTAL, ELEMENTAL LIFE SO WHEN AN EASIER EXISTENCE BECKONED NEARBY, THEY LEFT THEIR HOMES BEHIND THEM.

Island life – French style

Church bells chime as fishermen in slickers tend to their dories and uniformed gendarmes pace slowly by. The stop-you-in-your-tracks aroma of freshly baked baguettes fills the air and the clackety-clack of boys playing pelote basque echoes across the square. Locals kiss each other *bonjour*, and put petrol in their Citroëns that they pay for in Euros. This scene could be anywhere in France – except it is 3,819 km (2,373 miles) away across the North Atlantic.

St Pierre and Miquelon is a cluster of eight rugged islands that forms a self-governing

territory of France near Newfoundland. The islands were discovered by the Portuguese in 1520, nabbed by the British in 1763 and given to the French in 1816, in whose possession they have remained ever since. Although small, these islands were important because they gave France fishing rights to the Grand Banks off Newfoundland.

Today 5,500 people live on St-Pierre and 600 on Miquelon in a world that is culturally miles from, but geographically very close to, Newfoundland's fishing communities. The occasional cruise boat swings past these islands from afar, but there are few visitors. Those who do are rewarded with a little slice of France in North America and a prime view of one of the most windswept of all abandoned places: L'Île-aux-Marins.

Between a rock and a hard place

Its name translates as 'The Island of the Sailors', and it lies just 1 km (0.62 miles) away from St-Pierre across a choppy strait; a mere 15-minute ferry jaunt when wave and wind are favourable, but an impossible journey when a winter storm is raging.

L'Île-aux-Marins is tiny: just 1.5 km (0.93 miles) long and 400 m (1,310 ft) wide. Its highest point, Cape Beaudry, is only 35 m (115 ft) above mean sea level. Harsh winds have rendered it virtually treeless. It's harder to imagine a community sustaining life here than deciding to leave it. The island was first settled in 1604 and until the early

nineteenth century, its population grew in the same steady way as that of St-Pierre. Most of the fisherman had emigrated here from Brittany, Normandy, and the Basque country and by 1892 there was a thriving fishing community of 683 souls.

Luxury across the water

The settlement's decline was slow but inevitable. Throughout the early twentieth century the people were hit by several poor fishing seasons. Surviving on the bounty of the sea simply got too hard. Always visible across the water was the larger island of St-Pierre, which offered better-paid and more secure jobs, as well as shops, health care, schools and other facilities.

As the population dwindled in the 1950s and 1960s it got to a point where the community couldn't sustain itself. In 1965 the last families left for St-Pierre.

Since then, many of the buildings have been battered into dilapidation by Atlantic gales. However, several have been carefully preserved – to show what life was like here, in the teeth of the sea.

Lives of the fisher-folk

The Archipélitude Museum is located in the town's tiny school and has a unique collection of artefacts relating to the fishing industry and life on the islands. *La Maison Jézéquel* is a large (for the island) house that was once owned by the powerful fishing company *Morue Française* and now displays a fascinating collection of fishing tools and equipment.

Fishermen the world over take worship seriously, and the Church of Notre Dame des Marins (built in 1874) is the most striking building on the island. Its red roof stands proud of all other structures and is still occasionally used for special services. The cemetery is a poignant reminder of how dangerous a profession fishing is.

On the island's northeast shore lies the rusting wreck of a ship, the *Trans-pacific*; a skeleton that creeps slowly along the strand as it is buffeted by the strong gales and thumping waves that hit the island every year.

Windswept wonderland

Today, a few people stay on the island from May to November, in the handful of fishermen's homes that have been restored. They spend their time fishing, naturally, and offering basic services to the occasional tourists who visit in summer.

Not that the weather here is ever hot and balmy. Rough seas mean cancelled ferries, even in the height of the holiday season. In the chill wind and whipping rain it's easy to imagine the hardship and the insularity of life in centuries past.

Those who are lucky enough to make it out to the island will find that it doesn't take long to explore, but the fading reality of such a humble, peaceful existence stays with you for a long, long time.

Looking out over the channel towards the island of St-Pierre.

LEITH HARBOUR & GRYTVIKEN

Leith Harbour ○
Grytviken ○
SOUTH GEORGIA
(UK)

DATE ABANDONED	TYPE OF PLACE	LOCATION	REASON	INHABITANTS	CURRENT STATUS
1965	Whaling stations	South Atlantic Ocean	Economic	2,000	Dilapidated/ Colonized by wildlife

IN THE ICY ANTARCTIC OCEAN, MEN HUNTED THE WHALES THAT WERE PROCESSED INTO PRODUCTS TO BE FOUND IN EVERY HOUSEHOLD. WHILE WORKING THIS LONELY, UNPLEASANT JOB, THEY LIVED IN FAR-FLUNG OUTPOSTS NAMED AFTER HOME – BUT A LONG WAY FROM IT.

Life and death in a frozen ocean

The thin, fractured crescent of South Georgia drifts alone in the South Atlantic like a cast-off animal rib bone, hacked and chipped by the butcher's knife. The uninhabited South Sandwich Islands are the nearest neighbouring territory, lying 800 km (500 miles) southeast. The nearest civilization is on the Falkland Islands – but that is 1,390 km (864 miles) away to the west across the ice-cold ocean.

South Georgia has been a British possession since 1775 when Captain James Cook made the first circumnavigation and landing. It has never been home to an indigenous or even self-supporting population. The island is mostly taken up with two fearsome mountain ranges, with eleven peaks above 2,000 m (6,562 ft). Vast glaciers, ice caps and snowfields cover 75 per cent of its area even in summer. Its climate is polar and the weather harsh. In winter a shroud of thick snow envelops it right down to the iceberg-peppered sea. If there is an end to the earth, this is it.

Yet for several decades this was where 2,000 people lived, worked and prayed together, forming a thriving and profitable industry: the largest whaling centre on the planet.

The business of death

Whales were valuable. Their carcasses could be processed into several very useful materials. Whale oil was used in lamps (although it gave off a very unpleasant smell and was replaced with kerosene when that became cheap enough) and to make industrial-grade soap. It was also, for many years, the main ingredient in margarine. In 1933, 37 per cent of the fat in British margarines came from whales.

Whale oil was obtained by 'trying out' – boiling great strips of blubber flensed from the carcasses. If the whales were caught close to the

In its 58 years of operation, the whaling station at Grytviken on South Georgia handled 53,761 slaughtered whales.

FINAL PAGE: A sperm whale ready for flensing at Grytviken.

shore this was done on land, but on deep-sea expeditions, the trying-out was done on the ship itself.

With the flesh removed, the skulls and spines of whales were cut up by a steam saw and the pieces boiled to extract more oil. A good whale carcass could produce 29 tonnes of oil. The bones and waste products were then ground into bone meal to be used as fertilizer. Some whale meat for consumption was also produced.

The world's most remote industrial centre

Whaling companies first based themselves in the Falkland Islands, before moving to South Georgia to be closer to the whaling grounds. Every nail, brick, plank and girder of every whaling station building had to be brought from Europe to South Georgia by ship. Most buildings were prefabricated in Norway and then reassembled in sections.

The island was soon the world's biggest whaling centre, with seven main bases: Grytviken, Godthul, Ocean Harbour, Leith Harbour, Husvik Harbour, Stromness and Prince Olav Harbour. A small British administrative centre was built at King Edward Point near Grytviken. The name 'Grytviken' means 'Pot Bay' in Norwegian, a name earned in the nineteenth century when elephant seals were first boiled down here for oil.

From 1909–1965, Leith Harbour was the single busiest whaling station in the world. It housed 500 people who processed nearly 1,000 whales a year. Its neighbour at Grytviken handled 53,761 slaughtered whales in its 58 years of operation. In 1912, the largest whale ever caught was landed at Grytviken – a blue whale measuring 33.58 m (110 ft) long.

Incredibly, several of the stations had their own narrow gauge railway lines. Like the buildings themselves, every element of these railways had to be transported 13,000 km (8,000 miles) by sea. The trains were used to carry coal for the saws and blubber boilers, as well as heavy metal items such as harpoon heads. They helped transport the workers across the permafrost when it turned marshy in summer. The Grytviken railway system also carried the coffin of explorer Sir Ernest Shackleton on the way to its final resting place.

The largest and most successful whaling company was founded by a Norwegian immigrant to Scotland, Christian Salvesen. Starting as a shipping agent in Leith in 1872, he later diversified into the whaling industry and by 1914,

Salvesen's whaling fleet had two factory ships, five supply ships and eighteen whale catchers.

When the hard, dark Antarctic winter set in, the whale-catching ships in the Salvesen fleet would come into Leith Harbour (named after its Scottish counterpart) to be serviced. Engines were cleaned and oiled, new harpoons fitted to decks and flensing blades sharpened.

The slaughter dies off

In the twentieth century, whaling transformed from a labour- and time-intensive hunt to a highly mechanized and efficient harvest. Strong metal cables, cannon-fired harpoons and steam winches were mounted on fast, steam-powered ships. For the first time whalers could target the larger, swifter cetaceans with greater treasure in their bodies.

Factory ships were both the ultimate efficiency and the industry's death knell. When stern ramps were introduced in the late 1920s the factory ships could follow the whales into the remotest of waters and process them on board without the need to return to shore. This made the South Georgia stations increasingly redundant. It also meant that the whalers were now simply too good at their trade and were clearing the sea out as a result.

More than 50,000 whales a year were being killed in the late 1930s, far more than was sustainable, and by the end of the Second World War populations were significantly depleted. In 1946, the first quotas restricting international trade in whales were introduced, though these proved ineffective.

By the 1960s, Christian Salvesen's two whaling factory ships each had a hangar on board, with a Westland Whirlwind helicopter inside that was used for whale-spotting. (On a positive ecological note, his ships also brought home live penguins, making Edinburgh Zoo the first in the world to breed the birds.)

Blue whale hunting was banned in 1966, by which time 330,000 blue whales had been caught in the Antarctic – reducing the world's largest population of the animals to 0.15 per cent of its initial level.

By now vegetable oil had replaced whale oil in margarine, fertilizers were produced in a more efficient way, and the demand for whale products dropped off. The practice also became deeply unpopular and in 1986, the

International Whaling Commission banned commercial whaling altogether.

British whalers last worked here in the season 1960–1, when they processed 1,055 whales at Leith Harbour. A further 3,500 whales were caught and processed by Christian Salvesen's two factory ships. In 1965 the last whaling station was finally abandoned.

South Georgia today

A handful of the whaling station buildings have been actively preserved, such as the museum and church at Grytviken. There are no permanent human residents to develop the rest of the buildings or remove their contents, and so the general layouts of the sites are much as they were when the last whalers left. But the ferocious wind and driving precipitation have taken their toll on the buildings.

Fallen chimneys lie scattered at Stromness, by the very hut that Ernest Shackleton and his men trudged into after their death-defying walk across the island in 1916. Rusting harpoon barrels and screw propellers litter the foreshore.

The only inhabitants now are the local wildlife. Fur seals take up seasonal residence in the buildings of Leith Harbour. They move in early in the season and in summer they wage vicious, often fatal, fights for territory. The foreshore is littered with their carcasses and the battles make it too dangerous for photographers to explore the station.

Although cruise ships often visit the whaling bays, most of the buildings are now off-limits to visitors due to their decrepitude and the high levels of asbestos. To see inside the stations is to take a privileged step into a time machine. In many of the offices tallies of the numbers of whales caught are still pinned to the walls. Drawers of paperwork stand on desks ready to be audited. The site is a frozen snapshot of mid-twentieth century commercial life that just happens to have been transplanted to Antarctica.

WITTENOOM

Wittenoom
AUSTRALIA

DATE ABANDONED	TYPE OF PLACE	LOCATION	REASON	INHABITANTS	CURRENT STATUS
1966	Asbestos mine	Western Australia	Health hazard	500	Virtually abandoned/ Entry discouraged

FOR TWENTY YEARS ITS MINERAL RICHES MADE THIS A BOOM TOWN. BUT THAT VALUABLE MINERAL WAS ASBESTOS AND THE ENTIRE TOWN BECAME CONTAMINATED WITH TOXIC DUST. WITTENOOM IS SO DANGEROUS IT HAS BEEN DELETED FROM MAPS AND SCRUBBED OFF ROAD SIGNS.

The most dangerous town in the world

Some towns are dangerous because of their rough neighbourhoods. Others are perched on precipitous mountaintops or in the favoured paths of hurricanes. Wittenoom, however, is deadly because of the dust on the road, the rocks in the hills and the very air that blows through the streets. This was a town built around the mining of blue asbestos, at first considered one of the most useful of all minerals and now known to be the most toxic.

Humans have been aware of this fireproof fibrous crystal for at least 4,500 years. Bronze Age earthenware pots and cooking utensils strengthened with asbestos have been found in Finland. The word asbestos is from the ancient Greek for 'unquenchable' or 'inextinguishable'. Rich Persians stunned their guests by dropping a cloth made of asbestos into the fire to clean it. Marco Polo was shown *a good vein from which the cloth which we call of salamander, which cannot be burnt if it is thrown into the fire, is made . . .*.

Industrialization multiplied the number of uses for asbestos. By the end of the nineteenth century asbestos featured in concrete, bricks, pipe and fireplace cement, pipe insulation, ceiling insulation, fireproof drywall, flooring, roofing and even lawn furniture. In the Second World War, thousands of tonnes of asbestos were used in ships to insulate piping, boilers, steam engines, and steam turbines.

Crocidolite, or blue asbestos, has the best heat resistance. It has been used in spray-on coatings, pipe insulation, cement products and in millions of military gas masks – which is ironic, because this form of the mineral is also the most lethal.

The blue-rock boom

Blue asbestos was first found in the hills of the Hamersley Range in 1917. Mining began at Wittenoom Gorge in 1946 and proved so successful that a company town was built there the next year. The town attracted settlers and grew to a population of 500. Until the 1960s, Wittenoom was Australia's only asbestos mine, and its huge seams would go on to produce 161,000 tonnes of the valuable mineral. It was a true boom town.

However, it was only a matter of time before severe health problems surfaced. In the mines and mill, asbestos dust hung in the hot air like blue smoke. Clumps of the toxic mineral lay

OVERLEAF TOP:
The town was literally erased from the map.

OVERLEAF MIDDLE:
Visitors, other than kangaroos, are rare.

OVERLEAF BOTTOM:
A seam of blue asbestos (crocidolite) at Wittenoom.

scattered around the floor and every surface was coated a dirty blue. There were no extraction systems.

The danger wasn't just confined to the men who worked at the seams and in the processing buildings. Mine tailings were deliberately spread on the town's streets, the school playground and the local racetrack, to control the flyaway red dust that naturally covered the ground. Children could often be seen playing in the tailings, building castles in the blue-speckled sand. The town held competitions to see who could shovel a pile of tailings into a drum the fastest. Clouds of blue dust bloomed in the air as the bare-chested men shovelled themselves into a gasping sweat and onlookers cheered the victor.

For kids in the late 1950s and 1960s, exploring the old mine workings was a fun thing to do. Families travelling through Pilbara often stopped off to walk through the gorge, pick up rocks and check the mine openings for kangaroos.

The danger of denial

The dangers of asbestos have been known for almost as long as its benefits have. Pliny the Younger (AD 61–114) reported that slaves who worked with it became sick. The lethal danger of asbestos was confirmed by modern medicine in 1924 and eight years later the U.S. Bureau of Mines stated: 'It is now known that asbestos dust is one of the most dangerous dusts to which man is exposed.' The mineral was proven to be dangerous to mine, dangerous to manufacture with and dangerous to use. However, it remained in widespread use. Asbestos was useful, abundant, and there was then no viable alternative. It was also making a lot of people rich. The scientific discovery of the dangers and its subsequent suppression by the manufacturing parties were similar in form – and contemporaneous to – those of cigarette smoking.

Dust to dust

In Wittenoom there was a case of asbestosis the year the mine opened, and as early as 1948 doctors were warning of the catastrophic health problems that would occur. But there was no significant safety programme and nothing in the way of education. The workers and their families kept coming here, attracted by the good pay and community atmosphere.

However, the negative health reports increased. In the 1960s and 1970s the dangers of asbestos became front-page news worldwide, and its use was phased out. Wittenoom mine was closed in 1966, although this was influenced more by a sharp drop in profits than by health concerns. For most residents it was only after they had long departed Wittenoom that they began to fall ill.

As the compensation claims mounted, the severity of the danger became clear. From 1978 the town was phased down by the state government. The remaining residents were encouraged to leave and when they did their houses were demolished. By 1992, a third of the town's houses had been flattened. The school, nursing post, police station and airport were also soon closed.

The government finally cut the power and withdrew all services in 2006. The town was degazetted: removed from official maps and road signs. Warning signs were erected and roads that led to contaminated areas closed and dug up. Nevertheless, three die-hard residents remain (as of 2015). A few brave (or foolhardy) visitors also make the trip every year.

Exploring today

Wittenoom is 1,106 km (687 miles) north-northeast of Perth in the dry and sparsely populated Pilbara region. It isn't just the remoteness that makes Wittenoom hard to find: officially the town does not exist at all. The steps the authorities have taken to discourage entry are very effective. Many of the roads have been scrubbed up and bridges cut. Road signs have been altered or removed. If you do get close to the town then bright warning signs spell out the health risk loud and clear.

Wittenoom feels every inch like a ghost town. A diner that once thronged with hungry miners stands empty and unwelcoming. There are no cars to fill up at the garage's petrol pumps. There are a few pieces of mine equipment rusting in the bush, but the mine buildings themselves have gone. A few homes are still standing, scattered and lonely amid the poisonous tailings. There is also the sad sense that many more ghosts will soon haunt this place, thanks to the delayed death sentence of asbestos-related lung disease.

The deaths go on

The use of blue asbestos is now banned worldwide. Although white asbestos is banned or restricted in fifty-two countries, it is still mined today in Russia, China, Brazil, Kazakhstan and Canada. Around two million tonnes are produced every year, most of which go into fireproof cement for the booming building industries in India, Brazil, Thailand, Mexico, Pakistan, and the United Arab Emirates.

POVEGLIA

DATE ABANDONED	TYPE OF PLACE	LOCATION	REASON	INHABITANTS	CURRENT STATUS
1968	Quarantine island/Asylum	Italy	Disuse	Up to 6,000 patients	Abandoned

THE ISLAND LIES ONLY A FEW MINUTES BY VAPORETTO FROM THE GLORIES OF VENICE – BUT FEW BOATMEN WILL GO THERE. FOR CENTURIES THIS HAS BEEN A PLACE OF DEATH AND DISEASE, AND ITS REPUTATION LIVES ON TODAY.

On beauty's doorstep

On approach, Poveglia appears to be the most beautiful of all abandoned places. Drifting above the shimmering azure wavelets of the Venetian lagoon, it has lush trees, grassy slopes and elegant buildings nestling amid the greenery. Poking above the wooded canopy is a twelfth century bell tower that would be admired even were it amid Venice's architectural riches. This tiny settlement is surely a Benedictine monastery, a sanctuary of spiritual beauty outside the bustling city-state.

Yet all is not as it seems. This is an island where uncountable numbers of plague victims were brought to sicken, die and be cast into unmarked graves. For centuries there was little here but fear, pain and sadness. Even when the plague was no more, this was still a place of anguish. Within living memory, this was a secure psychiatric hospital, ruled by a doctor of cruel reputation and unsound practices.

Even now, the island's tragic past lives on in several macabre stories. It is said that so many people were cremated and buried here that the soil is 50 per cent human ash. Fishermen apparently avoid the area for fear of netting bones of their ancestors. These may just be the fevered imaginings of boatmen who saw the plague island rising out of the mists on a stormy night, or heard a scream of pain as they passed in a fog. However, what is certain is that despite its appealing exterior and multi-million dollar location, Poveglia remains utterly deserted to this day.

Island of sadness and horror

'The condition of the people was pitiable to behold. They sickened by the thousands daily, and died unattended and without help. Many died in the open street, others dying in their houses, made it known by the stench of their rotting bodies. Consecrated churchyards did not suffice for the burial of the vast multitude of bodies, which were heaped by the hundreds in vast trenches, like goods in a ships hold and covered with a little earth.'
Italian author Giovanni Bocaccio describing the Black Death

The fourteenth century outbreak of Black Death killed 30 per cent of the people in Europe. Venice was particularly vulnerable to infectious diseases: it ran an empire on sea trade, and there was a constant flurry of ships bearing cargo, and sailors, travelling from the most exotic corners of the world. The city pioneered plague prevention, appointing three guardians of public health during the first Black Death outbreak, in 1348.

Venice also established the first *lazaret*, a quarantine station for maritime travellers, in 1423. The word *quarantine* itself is Venetian in origin. It comes from the length of time travellers had to stay at a lazaret before they could pass into the city: *quaranta giorni*, or forty days.

By 1776, all ships arriving at Venice had to stop at Poveglia for a check by public health officials. When two ships carrying plague victims arrived in 1793, the island itself was designated a lazaret. It continued to perform this duty on and off until 1922 when it became a psychiatric asylum.

The hospital was finally closed in 1968. The outer garden-like section of Poveglia was run as a vineyard for a short time, but this too was soon abandoned.

The pits beneath the green

Seen from above, Poveglia is made up of three separate islands that form a wedge. The largest central section contains the buildings. The point of the wedge is formed by an octagonal fort; it was one of five built in 1645 by the Venetian government to guard the lagoon's entrances. This would have once been manned by soldiers and armed with cannon positioned behind high walls. Today it is merely a low earth rampart faced with brick, but its defensive shape is clearly visible. The outer section, reached by a bridge over a Venetian-style canal, is given over to nature. It is here that the plague pits are probably located.

It will never be known exactly how many infected people came to die on Poveglia, but researchers have calculated there could be as many as 100,000 bodies buried in its verdant outer section. That might sound like an exaggeration, but in the outbreak of 1576 alone, Venice lost 50,000 citizens. There were at least twenty-two more documented outbreaks of plague in the two centuries before that, and many more afterwards. Workers digging foundations on another quarantine island nearby – Lazaretto Vecchio – found 1,500 plague victims tightly packed into a single small grave pit.

Off limits, then and now

Very few people are lucky enough to explore the island: it remains state property and landings are strictly controlled by the Italian Government. Images brought back by those who have made it there show buildings with beautiful exteriors and decaying, very institutional interiors.

There is a covered shelter for boats, known as a *cavana*, and the hospital and asylum buildings still stand, albeit with the aid of some scaffolding. Other structures include the houses and offices once used by the hospital's staff. The bell tower was originally part of a church dedicated to San Vitale, but this was demolished on the orders of Napoleon Bonaparte in 1806. After that the bell tower was used as a lighthouse.

Wards and dormitories still contain beds, tables and chairs, now rusting. The handsome floor tiles at the rear of the psychiatric ward are cracked and greened with weeds. One room is deeply and completely carpeted with the torn-out pages of Italian books. In the laundry area, large rusty clothes driers line up against the wall. The hospital had its own chapel, which once featured a painting by the renowned Venetian artist Giovanni Tiepolo; but this has long gone. In some places, vines have blurred the distinction between inside and outside, pouring through broken windows and running their fingers round nearby furniture.

Ironically, the upstairs windows offer fabulous views of Venice and the even-closer Lido. This glamorous island playground is home to the Venice Casino, the Grand Hotel Excelsior and the Venice Film Festival. Every two years the most famous faces in the movie world are photographed here, often with Poveglia lurking in the background, its secrets still untold.

That is the sadness of Poveglia in a nutshell – that throughout the centuries the thousands of people condemned to end their days here have faced their doom knowing that they were within touching distance of one of humanity's most glorious and life-filled creations.

OVERLEAF: Poveglia island as seen from Malamocco, 700 m away across the Venetian lagoon.

CANFRANC STATION

FRANCE

Canfranc Station

SPAIN

DATE ABANDONED	TYPE OF PLACE	LOCATION	REASON	INHABITANTS	CURRENT STATUS
1970	Railway station	Pyrenees, Spain	Economic	10–20 staff	Abandoned

PERCHED HIGH IN THE PYRENEES IS A MIRACLE OF GLASS AND METAL – THE LARGEST RAILWAY STATION IN THE WORLD. ALAS, THIS MAGNIFICENT DREAM OF INTERNATIONAL EXCHANGE WAS UNDONE BY A SIMPLE ACCIDENT AND POLITICAL STAGNATION.

Death of a dream

On the wintry morning of 27 March 1970, a freight train inched out of Pau station in southern France heading for Zaragoza in Spain. However, as it climbed the steep Aspe Valley on its way to the France-Spain border that runs along the Pyrenees, the locomotive began to lose traction on the ice-bound rails. A mechanic got out to put sand down for extra grip, but found that the hoppers were empty. Then, in a perfect storm of misfortune, an electricity substation failed. The train lost even the power to stand still. It began rolling back down the line.

Out of control, it clipped a bridge at 100 km/h (60 mph) and instantly derailed. Iron wheels ripped up wooden sleepers. Screeching bogies buckled the track and in a second the nine wagons folded like a concertina. The momentum was unstoppable and the fragmenting train sliced its way clean through the bridge. The twisted mess of train and track ended up in the torrential Gave d'Aspe river. Miraculously, no one was killed; but the accident still had a disastrous consequence, for it put an end to one of the most beautiful railway journeys in the world.

Rails across the border

The concept behind the line was simple enough: to join the French region of Béarn and the Spanish region of Aragon with a railway line running north–south. But this meant traversing the Pyrenees. Although not as high as the Alps, this is still a mighty mountain range, extending 491 km (305 miles) from the Bay of Biscay all the way to the Mediterranean Sea and creating a natural barrier between France

and Spain. There are 129 summits over 3,000 m (9,843 ft) and the highest peak, Aneto, stands 3,404 m (11,168 ft) above sea level.

These mountains are mostly colossal slabs of granite and gneiss, hard rocks that have fared well against millennia of erosion. It took eighty bridges, twenty-four tunnels, four viaducts and a swathe of deforestation to take the railway line up the tightly curving Aspe Valley. This was extremely expensive: 50 per cent of the French section of the railway was built on engineered stone structures.

The engineering centrepiece of the international link was the cross-border tunnel. This took the line for 7.9 km (4.9 miles) beneath the Somport mountain pass with a slope reaching 4.7 per cent. It was begun in 1908, with the drilling teams meeting in the middle of the mountain four years later. Even then, it would still be another sixteen years before train services began.

Crossing the tracks
Spanish railway lines were originally built to a broader gauge than French lines, which used Standard Gauge. Today, trains can automatically switch between different gauges of track while on the move; but in the early twentieth century, passengers were forced to change trains. This meant that there had to be a transit station at the border, and on this line it would be an architectural jewel worthy of its incomparable mountain setting: Canfranc station.

The marvel in the mountains
With the route established, the vast frontier station now had to be created – at an elevation of 1,195 m (3,921 ft). An area of 18 hectares (44 acres) was cleared, with the River Aragón being diverted and new plantations of pine trees ranged on the slopes above to protect the railway from avalanches.

The station had to be big enough to process an entire train full of cross-border passengers at once. Furthermore, the station was on the Spanish side, and the creation of the building became a matter of national pride. Designed by Spanish architect Fernando Ramírez de Dampierre in a mix of classical and Art Nouveau styles, it was completed in 1928 and at the time was the largest train station in the world. The building was 240 m (787 ft) long with 300 windows and 156 doors.

There was a huge baggage hall, an infirmary for health checks and enough services to keep waiting passengers occupied. That meant waiting rooms, restaurants, bars, a currency exchange and a luxurious international hotel. The station building also housed offices, technical services and extensive staff accommodation.

French trains arrived on one side of Canfranc, and passengers exited directly into the mammoth station building. There they passed through customs and out onto a platform on the other side, where they boarded a Spanish train running on 'Iberian gauge'. The process ran in reverse the other way. Canfranc also had cranes, warehouses and a transporter bridge to transfer freight at the frontier.

On 18 July 1928, Canfranc International Station was inaugurated in the presence of Alfonso XIII, King of Spain,

and Gaston Doumergue, President of France. After more than 24 years of work, the Trans-Pyrenean route was in service. However, its working life would be just as fraught with difficulties as its construction.

Struggling to survive

The Pau–Zaragoza line had problems from the start. The severe demands asked of the engineers meant that the line was hounded by malfunctions. In a foreshadowing of the line's ultimate fate, a track defect caused a derailment at 1929 in Pont-Suzon.

There were also issues with the border transfer at Canfranc. Travellers reported huge queues at customs, with hours of waiting. The 311 km (193 mile) journey between Pau and Zaragoza took a whole day to complete; and even after that, on the French side there were no simple connections from Pau to Bordeaux or Paris.

Freight and passenger traffic was almost immediately hit by the economic depression of 1929 and the majestic station was badly damaged by fire in 1931. The Spanish Civil War broke out five years later and the border was closed.

Spain was officially neutral in the Second World War, but that didn't stop the line being used for military purposes. General Franco's regime had received considerable German assistance in the Civil War, and the favour was repaid. After the fall of Paris in 1940, convoys of iron and tungsten ore from Galicia travelled through to boost the German war machine. Discoveries made in 2000 showed that 86.6 tonnes of Nazi gold had travelled the other way, from Switzerland through to Spain and Portugal.

Post-war decline

In 1948 trans-Pyrenean traffic was resumed, but the line suffered from lack of investment and, in particular, power supply problems. After the accident in 1970, the SNCF (the French National Rail Company) had the perfect pretext to close the line and avoid extensive, expensive repairs. Although the site of the destroyed bridge was low down in the valley and easily accessible, it was never rebuilt and trains terminated at Bedous. A bus service then ran up to Canfranc. After forty-two years of service, this wonderful international railway journey had reached the end of the line.

The station today

The French side of Canfranc Station is completely abandoned and overgrown. On the Spanish side, two little railcars still run a local service from Zaragoza. There are tourist services in July and August and the odd freight train occasionally arrives. A pressure group has long campaigned for the re-establishment of the link and in recent years this has looked more likely to happen. With the bulk of the beautiful building still extant, this is one abandoned place that may again – some day – be filled with human life.

EASTERN STATE PENITENTIARY

DATE ABANDONED	TYPE OF PLACE	LOCATION	REASON	INHABITANTS	CURRENT STATUS
1971	Prison	Pennsylvania, USA	Outdated	450 prisoners & dozens of staff	Historic landmark

The barber's chair still waits for customers.

THIS WAS THE REVOLUTIONARY FORTRESS-PRISON WHERE GUILTY MEN AND WOMEN SPENT THEIR LIVES IN CONSTANT SOLITARY CONFINEMENT. THE DEEDS OF THE MOST HARDENED OF CRIMINALS MAY NOW BE FORGOTTEN, BUT THEY ARE EASILY IMAGINED WHEN WALKING THESE COLD STONE CORRIDORS.

The monstrous model prison

The gatehouse is a huge castle-like structure built of gloomy stone. From either side sheer, looming walls 9 m (30 ft) high stretch out to distant turreted corners. Within, out of sight from all but the birds, is a prison where 450 people lived and died without ever seeing or speaking to one another.

For in this prison, solitary confinement was the norm. All day, every day, the prisoners were locked alone inside their 2.4 m (8 ft) wide, 3.7 m (12 ft) long and 3 m (10 ft) high cells. By today's standards this seems like a cruel and unpleasant place to put people, but this was actually a radical social experiment aimed at revolutionizing the way that crime was dealt with.

When the Eastern State Penitentiary was completed in 1829 it was the largest and most expensive public structure ever built. The vast complex covered a 4.5 hectare (11 acre) site outside Philadelphia.

Crime, punishment and rehabilitation

Then, as now, this colossal edifice was a tourist attraction. Charles Dickens, a man who knew from personal experience how miserable prison life could be (his father had been jailed), visited when he toured America. In contrast to other contemporary correctional institutions, where forced labour and physical punishment were the norm, the concept behind Eastern State was the quiet contemplation of one's sins. The Quakers who established its philosophy believed that with enough solitude to ruminate on their transgressions, the prisoners would eventually change their outlook and habits. They would become penitent.

The prison's British architect, John Haviland, created a foreboding neo-Gothic exterior to deliberately intimidate any passers-by who might entertain the thought of committing a crime. Seven spoke-like cell blocks radiated out from a central hub where guards watched all from a high control tower. This radial floor plan and system of solitary confinement became a template for more than 300 prisons worldwide.

Each cell had a single window, nicknamed 'the eye of God'. The cells were small but had a tap, heating, a toilet (flushed remotely, twice a week) and individual exercise yards. The penitentiary had running water before the White House did.

There were no communal areas and although the prisoners lived alone in their cells, every inmate was visited once a day by the warden – and three times by overseers – to help guide their rehabilitation.

After being followed for nearly 100 years, the solitary confinement rule was abolished in the early twentieth century; overcrowding had made it a physical impossibility. The prison was expanded by the addition of a further eight new blocks (one of them designed by an inmate) to the seven spokes of the original wagon wheel.

The ideals are compromised

This did not necessarily mean there was an improvement in conditions for the inmates: the guards still regularly drenched prisoners in icy water in winter, bound them into chairs with leather straps and beat them, or kept them isolated in the 'Hole' – a lightless pit in the cellar – for weeks at a time.

Eastern State Penitentiary may have been ominous, but it was not escape-proof. One group of prisoners scaled the walls using homemade ladders, and in April 1945, twelve inmates used a 30 m (97 ft) tunnel to get under the prison wall and flee. It had taken them a year to dig. When the prison was renovated in the 1930s, thirty more incomplete tunnels were found.

The prison was closed in January 1970, when the cost of repairing the old buildings was considered too high, and the inmates were transferred to other institutions. The facility temporarily housed inmates the following year, after a riot in another prison nearby – but after that it fell into dereliction. For twenty years it lay abandoned, vegetation and a colony of feral cats taking over. Then, in the early 1990s it was established as a museum in a state of preserved decay.

Today visitors can explore the eerie and unpleasant cell blocks, with their narrow corridors and oppressive vaulted ceilings. Some cell blocks remain closed to the public and in here are fascinating insights into ordinary lives of men and women in captivity: worn-down shoes, well-thumbed magazines and stacked rolls of decades-old toilet paper still sit in the long-vacant cells.

Most haunted

There were no executions here: those prisoners who were on Death Row were taken elsewhere to meet their maker. However, plenty of men did die within these walls, of old age, violence, disease and, on several occasions, at the hands of the guards. It's not surprising that the penitentiary's bloody history and its ghostly atmosphere have led to the telling of some exuberant ghost stories.

Curiously, one cell shows off a coloured extravaganza of luxury items: a scroll-backed armchair upholstered in fine-striped cotton; an oriental rug; potted plants; elegant shaded lamps; an antique desk with a glass-fronted bookcase above it and a couple of replica Old Master oil paintings. In 1929 this incongruous oasis of high living was home to the gangster Alphonse 'Al' Capone.

VAROSHA

CYPRUS ○Varosha

DATE ABANDONED	TYPE OF PLACE	LOCATION	REASON	INHABITANTS	CURRENT STATUS
1974	Holiday resort	Cyprus	War	39,000	Abandoned/ Under military guard

THE SUN STILL SHINES ON THE BEACHES, BUT HOLIDAYMAKERS ARE UNLIKELY EVER TO COME HERE AGAIN. ONE OF THE MEDITERRANEAN'S MOST FABULOUS RESORTS WAS TURNED INTO A MINED AND FENCED NO-MAN'S-LAND ALMOST OVERNIGHT BY A VICIOUS ETHNIC CONFLICT.

Paradise in peril

Imagine you are staying in a luxury hotel in one of the world's most glamorous beach resorts: Koh Samui, Miami Beach or St Tropez. From your balcony you gaze out over an elegant golden crescent of sand, lapped by turquoise waters. Parasols made from palm leaves shade a scattering of sun loungers. A frisson of excitement ripples through the cool marble-tiled hotel bar: the planet's most famous movie-star couple are sipping drinks by the pool. As the sun blisters the horizon in a rosy farewell to another idyllic day, the holiday atmosphere is complete. Then, the next morning, you arise and step out onto your balcony to find the entire resort around you is utterly deserted.

It sounds like a scenario from a science fiction movie, but this is exactly what happened to Varosha, Cyprus, in 1974.

The colonial corner of the 'Med'

Cyprus enjoys 326 days of sunshine a year and is blessed with a multitude of beautiful beaches. The 1960s boom in jet travel saw huge growth in many Mediterranean resorts, and Cyprus was particularly well placed to capitalize on this new wave of visitors. Varosha, previously the Greek Cypriot quarter of Famagusta, was actively developed as a tourist destination. It soon became the most famous resort in Cyprus and one of the most popular in the world.

Varosha was A-list glamorous. Elizabeth Taylor and Richard Burton, Brigitte Bardot and Raquel Welch could be spotted relaxing on the patios and soaking up the Mediterranean sun. (Taylor's favourite bolthole was the Argo Hotel on JFK Avenue, a wide street studded with high-rise hotels.)

Boutiques, bars and luxury car dealerships stood side-by-side with ramshackle old cafés serving homely Greek fare. Citrus groves were replaced with swimming pools. As well as a lively flow of foreign visitors, there were 39,000 full-time residents.

But what most sun worshippers didn't know, or at least had no reason to acknowledge, was that the political situation was not as peaceful as the waters that lapped the beach.

Politics behind the palm trees

Cyprus is 240 km (150 miles) long and 100 km (62 miles) wide. It covers an area slightly smaller than Northern Ireland and has been equally

riven by political and religious conflict. With Turkey to the north, Greece to the west, Syria and Lebanon to the east, and Israel and Egypt further south, it is not surprising that Cyprus has had its sovereignty scrabbled over for centuries.

Cyprus was annexed by Britain in 1914, after 300 years of Ottoman rule, and became a Crown colony. In the 1950s Greek unionists led a guerrilla war against British occupation, and in 1960 the island gained independence. The Greek and Turkish communities agreed on a constitution, but cultural and ideological differences still ran very deep. This caused conflict, and a United Nations peace-keeping force was set up in 1964.

At this point, the first buffer zone between the Greek and Turkish communities was established. The line was drawn by Major General Peter Young, the commander of the peace force. Young drew his ceasefire line on a map of Cyprus using a dark green crayon, and since then the dividing frontier has been called the 'Green Line'.

The 1974 coup and Turkish invasion

Archbishop Makarios III, the Cypriot president, was elected in January 1968 on the platform of an independent Cyprus. But neighbouring Greece was then ruled by a military junta that saw Cyprus as the perfect stage for its ideological and territorial ambitions. Most officers in the Cypriot National Guard were Greek regulars who supported the junta. On 15 July 1974 the National Guard, with the backing of the Greek military junta, organized a coup d'état in Cyprus. They deposed President Makarios III.

Just five days later Turkish military forces invaded Cyprus. This was a full-scale assault, with troops landing on the beaches, tanks rumbling through the streets and air strikes throwing up plumes of fire and shattered concrete. Many buildings in Varosha were toppled by bombs dropped from Turkish aircraft.

To the cocktail-sipping holidaymakers the violence came straight out of the blue and they scrambled to evacuate. By August, Turkish forces controlled 40 per cent of the island. An uneasy ceasefire was declared and the island effectively partitioned along the Green Line. In the face of all-out war with Turkey, the Greek military junta collapsed and was replaced by a democratic government.

But for most islanders their lives were turned completely upside down. After the invasion, 165,000 Greek Cypriots (a quarter of the island's population) either fled, or were driven from, the Turkish-occupied north. Around 55,000 Turkish Cypriots went the other way soon after.

When the Turkish and Greek Cypriot armies were poised to do bloody battle in the streets of Famagusta, the Greek population of Varosha fled with just the clothes on their backs to avoid an almighty slaughter. However, this exodus was only ever meant to be temporary. When the violence had blown over they would return. Surely such a thriving city could not simply be snuffed out?

But Varosha's reputation as a paradise for millionaires and movie stars had gone up in a puff of grenade smoke.

No-man's-land

The Greek population took refuge to the south in the towns of Paralimni and Larnaca, and the Turkish military fenced off Varosha as soon as it was captured. The tourist town became a part of the buffer zone of the Green Line. Former residents were never allowed to return and all visits – except those by military personnel – were forbidden.

Varosha is still visible from Famagusta. The same sun shines on the two resorts, the same cool blue waves lap the same sand; but while the northern resort flourishes, Varosha remains desolate.

The resort today

In 1984 the UN ruled that Varosha should only be resettled by pre-invasion inhabitants. This meant that Turkey could not reopen the town as a resort. However, Turkey was disinclined to simply hand it back. A stalemate settled over the ghost town.

Even if the political differences could be put aside, it is now too late for Varosha. Decay is everywhere. Remedial work would be far too expensive. It would now be a case of bringing in the bulldozers and starting again – and even that would be more costly than simply starting again somewhere else.

And so the millionaires' playground lies vacant and fenced off, unlikely ever to reopen. The only visitors now are bored Turkish soldiers patrolling the dusty, cracked streets looking for trespassers. They are authorized to arrest and even shoot persons found illegally venturing into the town. This makes photographs of the ruins very rare indeed.

Those images that have emerged show hotel rooms abandoned with luggage on the bed and toothbrushes on the bathroom shelf. Wardrobes stand full of clothes. Tables are still set for dinner. A construction crane spikes the skyline above a hotel it never finished building. Car showrooms are full of models fresh off the 1974 factory line – wipe off the dust and their paintwork shines.

While the resort has become uninhabitable to man, the streets have been reclaimed by nature. A family of birds nests in a hotel fountain. Vines thrive in a sunlit corner of a long-closed restaurant. Sea turtles are the only souls on beaches once thronged with sunbathers. So the plants and animals live on, undisturbed in their very own holiday paradise.

HASHIMA ISLAND

JAPAN

○Hashima Island

DATE ABANDONED	TYPE OF PLACE	LOCATION	REASON	INHABITANTS	CURRENT STATUS
1974	Coal mining community	Japan	Economic	5,000	Abandoned

IT SEEMS TO BE CUTTING THROUGH THE WAVES LIKE A MIGHTY BATTLESHIP, BUT THIS WAS ACTUALLY ONE OF THE MOST DENSELY POPULATED SETTLEMENTS ON EARTH – A VERITABLE FORTRESS THAT OWED ITS EXTRAORDINARY EXISTENCE TO A DANGEROUS COAL MINE RUNNING DEEP BENEATH THE SEA FLOOR.

The gateway to hell

Hashima is known as Battleship Island (Gunkanjima) in Japanese, and this nickname certainly fits. Seen on approach from the ocean it seems to be ploughing through the waves, a long low prow, short stern and a cluster of structures amidships. The illusion must have been even more complete forty years ago when several chimneys belched smoke into the air like funnels.

The island is tiny, just 480 m (1,575 ft) long and 160 m (525 ft) wide – roughly equivalent to four football stadiums. Yet, within living memory, this inhospitable-looking rock was the most densely populated place on earth.

In 1959, a census indicated that over 5,000 people lived here. This little isle was like a place from Greek mythology: a twisting labyrinth of densely populated streets swarming with bodies, which surrounded a hole into the very earth itself. What's more, this gouge into the guts of the planet was continually growing, with the ejected slag being used to reclaim land from the sea.

A symbol of Japan's rapid industrialization

By the start of the twentieth century Japan had become Asia's first industrialized nation and a rising military power. Industrialization increased demand for coal and there was a dramatic rise in production. Japan's first modern mine had been sunk on Takashima Island, very close to Hashima, in 1868. This was a joint venture between Lord Nabeshima of Saga and the Scotsman Thomas Glover, who also helped found the Mitsubishi Corporation.

Mitsubishi was established as a shipping company in 1870. It soon diversified to serve its own needs: ships needed coal so it sunk mines; it bought a shipbuilding yard to make its own repairs; purchasing an iron mill made sourcing raw materials cheaper.

Coal was first discovered on the rocky reef of Hashima in 1810, but the first mine wasn't sunk until 1887. Mitsubishi bought the mine in 1890 when it was still a mere outcrop; but as spoil from the mine was discarded around the island, and engineers built a series of revetments, the island was progressively enlarged.

Hashima was the coal mining equivalent of an oil rig. Four shafts were sunk deep into the island, burrowing as much as 1 km (3,280 ft) below the sea floor. There were elaborate subterranean facilities to extract the coal, after which it was cut and cleaned underground then brought up and taken to a storage depot on a conveyor belt, ready for collection by ship and transport to steel refineries. The coal dug up from beneath Hashima was of excellent quality. It supplied the large steel works in Yahata, directly driving

Japan's rapid industrialization. Meanwhile the workers, and their families, clung on to an existence around the very pit-head itself.

By 1959 a total of 5,259 people called this home; a density of 835 people per 10,000 square metres. At its peak, it had the equivalent of 65,737 people per square kilometre. This made it 150 per cent more densely populated than the world's current most densely populated city, Manila in the Philippines, which has 42,857 people per square kilometre.

Life on Hell Island

'The digging places were so small that we had to crouch down to work. It was excruciating, exhausting labour. Gas collected in the tunnels, and the rock ceilings and walls threatened to collapse at any minute. I was convinced that I would never leave the island alive.'

Suh Jung-Woo, a Korean forced to work at Hashima

Life as a miner at Hashima was brutal, dangerous and not willingly undertaken. During the Second World War, many Chinese and Korean prisoners of war were used as forced labour here. To them, Hashima was known as 'Hell Island'.

Many of the coal faces were 1,000 m (3,280 ft) underground, where the temperature topped 45°C. Seawater constantly seeped into the pits, and there were dangerous ingresses of methane. Workers suffered from malnutrition, exhaustion and infections, with often at least one dying every week.

The bodies were ferried to the neighbouring island of Nakanoshima to be buried. Of the 500 Koreans who worked on the island between 1939 and 1945, 120 died there.

Indeed, Hashima is so ominous and threatening that it earned a starring role as the lair of James Bond villain Raoul Silva, in the 2012 film *Skyfall*.

The arrival of the atomic age

On 9 August 1945 the residents had an uncomfortably close view of one of the modern world's greatest tragedies – when the United States dropped the 'Fat Man' atomic bomb on Nagasaki, just 15 km (9 miles) away.

The blast wave shattered windows and damaged some buildings on Hashima. Korean and Chinese labourers were brought here and forced to clean up the rubble of the atomic explosion, exposing them to dangerous levels of radiation.

Conditions did improve after the war. In 1958, the island was the first place in Japan to have television sets and refrigerators. In the 1960s and early 1970s, the island had its own cinema and supermarket.

Day to day living

A points system determined the quality of the housing allotted to workers. Length of employment and status

within the company determined which floor the workers lived on. The higher up the better: lower floors got swamped during typhoons. A typical high-rise block had 317 families living in it.

The Nikkyu apartments block was built from reinforced concrete just after the First World War. It had 241 rooms, and at nine storeys high it was then the tallest building in Japan.

Hashima's school had seven floors and was the last building to be constructed on the island. The lunch hall had the island's only lift – which was used for transporting meals rather than children. The school closed for the final time on 31 March 1974. The children gathered in groups in the playground to form the words 'Sayonara Hashima'.

Spirituality was of great importance to the miners who risked their lives every day, so there was a temple with a shrine. Every year on 3 April, the entire population would gather to celebrate the shrine's 'Yamagami Festival'.

The coal fires die out

In 1941 a record 411,000 tonnes of coal was mined at Hashima. As a nation, Japan's peak coal production year was 1960, with a total of 55 million tonnes. But domestic coal was becoming increasingly expensive to extract compared with imported coal. Petroleum increasingly replaced coal

as a power source, and Japan opened the first of many nuclear power stations in 1966.

In December 1973 the order was given to close the pit. The Mitsubishi Company offered workers new jobs on the mainland – on a first come, first served basis. This was a simple motivational strategy to encourage the residents to leave quickly. It worked. The mine officially closed on 15 January 1974 and within six months the last living soul had departed from Hashima.

Many of the residents left in such a rush that in places it appears the evacuation almost took place overnight. In a hospital ward, X-ray photographs lie scattered on the floor, the images of miners' lungs not yet faded. A barber's shop has chairs ready for customers. A banking hall maintains its solemn formality. The shrine still stands, as do several restaurants, dotted with empty sake bottles, and the school – in one classroom the name of the teacher is still chalked on the blackboard. Exercise books, rusting tricycles, a broken abacus; even lone shoes lie on ruined pathways, as if lost in the headlong haste to escape the island.

TATOOINE

DATE ABANDONED	TYPE OF PLACE	LOCATION	REASON	INHABITANTS	CURRENT STATUS
1976–2003	Film set	Tunisia	Temporary use	Crews of several hundred	Abandoned/Some restoration

oTatooine
TUNISIA

GEORGE LUCAS CHOSE THE SAHARA DESERT IN TUNISIA TO DOUBLE AS LUKE SKYWALKER'S HOME PLANET IN *STAR WARS*. AFTER FILMING, THE CREW SIMPLY WALKED AWAY FROM THIS REMOTE SET. TODAY IT REMAINS A LITTLE PIECE OF A GALAXY FAR, FAR AWAY, HERE ON EARTH.

RIGHT: Luke Skywalker's homestead is a ruin.

FAR RIGHT: The *Star Wars* set at Chott el Gharsa, Tunisia.

Alien life on Earth

Tiny doors carved into sun-scorched rock; whitewashed, domed houses; strange electronic antennae; arched galleries cut into cliffs and half-filled with sand – this settlement looks like a place from another world. If it also seems familiar, that's because some of the most memorable scenes in modern movie history were filmed here. This is the set that depicted Luke Skywalker's home planet in the *Star Wars* films.

The movie's young hero lived on Tatooine, a barren world with twin suns. After a lengthy scout of locations that included all American, North African, and Middle Eastern deserts, director George Lucas cast the endless dunes and saltpans of the Tunisian Sahara in the role of this alien planet. In 1976 the *Star Wars* film crew arrived and began an eight-week process of transforming the isolated desert into a fantastic, otherworldly environment. Conditions were challenging, with temperatures topping 57°C and freak rainstorms threatening to wash out production.

They worked their magic in several locations. The Lars Homestead, where Luke gazed up at his planet's twin suns, was filmed on Chott el Djerid, the Sahara's largest saltpan. The interior scenes were shot in real-life underground dwellings at Matmata, so the crew dug some craters next to the little igloo, to create the illusion of an underground structure in the movie. A dry gulley at Sidi Bouhel, 23 km (14 miles) northeast of Tozeur featured prominently in the film and was nicknamed 'Star Wars Canyon'. This location was also used in *Raiders of the Lost Ark* and in *The English Patient*. Obi-Wan Kenobi's house was a storage hut once used by fishermen on the island of Djerba.

At the end of the two-and-a-half week shoot, the crew decided to simply leave the sets where they were. This was partly due to the site's extreme remoteness: no one from the local government minded that the sets were left, and they would probably disintegrate quickly. There they would remain, untouched

and unvisited for twenty-one years.

New developments on Tatooine

George Lucas and his crew returned to Tunisia in 1997 to shoot scenes for *The Phantom Menace*, the first of the 'prequel' trilogy of *Star Wars* films. Two decades of desert wind and sand had taken their toll on the plywood and fibreglass structures, so the set designers carefully repaired them ready for another round of filming.

They also built a lavish new set from scratch in the desert northwest of the city of Tozeur. This would represent Mos Espa, the birthplace of Anakin Skywalker, the character who would become Darth Vader. Again, when filming wrapped, the buildings were left intact where they had been built.

A planet rediscovered online

Like the sets from the first films, these later constructions were left at the mercy of the desert. Then, in 2010, New York-based photographer Ra di Martino was using *Google Maps* to look at Chott el Djerid when she noticed someone had posted a picture of a crumbling movie set. She discovered that many movie studios have left sets behind in the desert, so she began trying to track down the lost buildings of *Star Wars*. In-depth research gave her several clues as to the sets' exact locations. She then used *Google Maps* and a local driver as guides and set off into the vast desert plains to find the abandoned towns of Tatooine.

Di Martino found sets in three locations, including Luke's original home and the extensive buildings of Mos Espa. Almost this entire town still stands, including the entrance gates, the pod-racing arena, and streets featuring Watto's shop, the market and Sebulba's café. The wind has torn at the fibreglass shells of the buildings, and sand fills the doorways, but there is much that looks exactly as it does on screen. Minus the aliens, of course.

Following their rediscovery, the sets have become a place of pilgrimage for intrepid fans. They have proved to be an unexpected and welcome attraction in a country still reeling from the dramatic wave of social and political unrest of 2010–11. In 2012, some *Star Wars* fans even raised funds to restore Luke's windblown house.

However, anyone wanting to visit Mos Espa will need to act soon. Since filming of the third film in the prequel trilogy was completed in 2003, the Saharan dunes have been encroaching on the film set at the rate of 4 cm (1.5 inches) per day. Soon, this alien city will be lost beneath the sands of planet earth.

TOP LEFT: The sets are now owned by the Tunisian Government.

BOTTOM LEFT: The 'stone' buildings are actually fibreglass on wooden frames.

SANZHI UFO HOUSES

Sanzhi O
UFO Houses

TAIWAN

DATE ABANDONED	TYPE OF PLACE	LOCATION	REASON	INHABITANTS	CURRENT STATUS
1980	Holiday homes	Taiwan	Economic	c. 100 tourists	Redevelopment

FUN, COLOURFUL AND ODDLY ALIEN, THESE POD-LIKE BUILDINGS WERE A 1970s VISION OF THE HOLIDAY HOMES OF THE FUTURE. SADLY, THEIR BOLD ARCHITECTURE WAS NOT APPRECIATED IN ITS TIME, AND THEY FELL VICTIM TO HARSH COASTAL CONDITIONS.

Two of the multicoloured apartment blocks.

Space age holidays are here

They look like they have just landed from space, but these pod houses were built as earthly holiday homes in Taiwan.

They were constructed in 1978 at a location blessed with panoramic sea views just 15 km (9 miles) from the capital, Taipei City. Taiwan had by this time recovered from the oil crisis of the early 1970s and was enjoying a new economic boom. The mood in the country was generally optimistic and people were keen to look to the future. Their space age design is understandable, given that Star Wars had just broken box office records worldwide.

The pod houses were to be just one part of an extensive resort that also had water slides and swimming pools. The developer hoped to rent them out to US military personnel on furlough from their East Asian postings. There were around 50,000 US troops in Japan at the time, 28,000 Americans in South Korea, while both the US Air Force and the US Navy had their largest overseas base in the Philippines. Taiwan lies roughly in the middle of these three countries, so the business idea behind the pod houses was, in theory, a good one.

Life after death

However, the soldiers and airmen failed to see the attraction of the site, and few, if any, visited. The developer ran out of money before the complex was finished. The houses that had been built were completely abandoned just two years after construction.

The wind and ocean spray soon took its toll on the bright paintwork and broad windows. This decay only seemed to add to the attraction of their extraordinary architecture however, and the pod-like structures enjoyed a new lease of life as a favourite haunt of urban explorers, tourists, photographers and filmmakers.

This new life would not last long. Despite an online petition to save the buildings, or even just to preserve one of them as a museum, developers razed the site to make way for what they described as a 'more normal' seaside resort and water park. As of 2010, every one of the pod houses had been destroyed – sent back to the great mother ship in the sky.

MILLENNIUM MILLS

DATE ABANDONED	TYPE OF PLACE	LOCATION	REASON	INHABITANTS	CURRENT STATUS
1981	Flour mill	London's docklands	Economic	Hundreds of employees	Abandoned

IT WAS ONCE THE LARGEST AND MOST ADVANCED BUILDING OF ITS TYPE IN THE WORLD. NOW IT IS A RUINED ANACHRONISM, A CRUMBLING INDUSTRIAL SHELL SURROUNDED BY THE REDEVELOPED GLAMOUR OF LONDON'S DOCKLANDS.

ABOVE: Across the dock from the derelict mills are modern offices and exhibition centres.

OVERLEAF: Spiralling chutes for bags of flour and a more recent addition, a modern mural by street artist Shepard Fairey, which at time of creation was the largest work of street art in the UK.

A building out of time

The Millennium Mills are a dark heart amid the flashing glass and steel of London's docklands. Now abandoned for more than three decades, these rotting mills stand in stark contrast to the fast-developing world around them.

Private jets swoop into the clouds from London City Airport, which lies on the edge of the next dock, just 500 m (1,640 ft) to the east. The technologically marvellous Thames Barrier waits to save the city from flooding on the river to the south. Futuristic technology is regularly on display just a few metres across the water in the ExCel exhibition centre. In every other corner of the docklands there are expensive offices, smart flats and the smooth, driverless trains of the Docklands Light Railway. Inside the mills however, there is only industrial ruin.

They are, however, just as much a monolith to money as any of the office towers in Canary Wharf.

ABOVE: The mills in 1934.

A dock worthy of a world empire

The Royal Victoria Dock was originally gouged out of raw marshland in 1850 and was built on a huge scale – it was the first London dock that could berth large steam ships. The dock was a runaway success, and within ten years it was handling four times as much cargo as the older docks

to the west. London was the heart of the world's greatest empire and there was a seemingly inexorable growth in trade.

Two more huge docks were built to the east, and around the turn of the twentieth century a series of mills were constructed here. First came the Silvertown Confectionery Mill, then the Premier Flour Mill in 1904 and finally the gargantuan Millennium Mills a year later. These three mills were the flagship enterprises of the largest milling companies in the United Kingdom and, indeed, in the whole of the British Empire.

Grain came up the Thames on ships, to be unloaded by cranes on the wharf and processed into flour by these giant mills that stood right on the quayside. In Millennium Mills' heyday, its hundreds of workers and floor upon floor of machines were able to process 100 sacks per hour. The flour was loaded onto trains and whisked away to bakers and shops all over the country.

A bang ends the boom
In 1917, however, an explosion at a nearby munitions factory badly damaged the mill's grain stores and silos. Millennium Mills wasn't rebuilt until 1933, when it took its current form – a 10-storey Art Deco building. The Luftwaffe dropped thousands of tonnes of bombs on London's docks during the Second World War, and the mills took several direct hits.

With Hitler vanquished it was back to business as usual – but only after a major reconstruction of the docks and the mills; it was 1953 before the mills were back at full production. They continued operating for nearly thirty more years, but by 1981 the economic landscape had changed for good and the Royal Docks were closed. The mills that stood on them were also put to sleep.

A rotting shell by the river
In many places the wooden floors are completely rotted through, revealing a skeleton of iron beams. Between these metal limbs are sudden deadly drops – yawning abysses up to ten floors deep.

Many of the holes were made when machinery was taken out to be salvaged for scrap. Where the ironwork was too large or cumbersome to be removed, it has been left in situ.

Higher still, one final series of steps lead up to the roof door… or at least they did, once. Precipitation leaking from above has taken its toll on the wooden beams, reducing this final staircase to little more than a soggy mush. It's worth the journey, though: the view from the top is jaw-dropping, with the towers of Canary Wharf glinting in the sun and the mighty river meandering to the sea.

The machines stop turning
By the 1990s many of the dock-related businesses had relocated to the docks further downstream at Tilbury. Most of the dockside buildings were demolished by the London Docklands Development Corporation, as part of the regeneration programme that saw huge areas of derelict docklands converted to residential, commercial and light industrial use. Only one silo survived at Millennium Mills, thanks to Grade II listing; two others fell to the wrecking ball.

A massive redevelopment project was approved in 2007, which would transform these 24 hectares (59 acres) into a new urban centre; the older mills would be demolished as the Millennium building was converted into a block of 400 luxury flats. The economy woes of 2008 stalled progress, and the project was officially cancelled in February 2010.

In 2015 it looked like the gigantic building was finally going to be granted a new lease of life. The Mayor of London announced a £12 million funding package to help convert Millennium Mills into a centre for start-up businesses. There will be a new bridge to connect Silvertown Quays with the Crossrail station at Custom House, and the building itself will be converted into apartments and business units. It would be fitting if at least one of these new businesses was a bakery…

BUZLUDZHA MONUMENT

DATE ABANDONED	TYPE OF PLACE	LOCATION	REASON	INHABITANTS	CURRENT STATUS
1989	Communist monument	Bulgaria	Ideological	0	Abandoned

IT WAS ONCE A GATHERING PLACE FOR INFLUENTIAL COMMUNIST FIGURES, AN AMBITIOUS SYMBOL OF NATIONALISM AND REVOLUTION THAT STOOD SENTINEL ABOVE THE SLOPES WHERE THOUSANDS OF BULGARIANS DIED FOR THEIR COUNTRY'S FREEDOM. NOW ITS CREED AND CONCRETE ARE ALIKE IN RUINS AND THE MONUMENT HAS BECOME AN UNLIKELY TOURIST HOTSPOT.

**'ON YOUR FEET
DESPISED COMRADES
ON YOUR FEET YOU SLAVES OF LABOUR!
DOWNTRODDEN AND HUMILIATED
STAND UP AGAINST THE ENEMY!'**

These rousing words are written on the wall of a vast monument that stands alone on an elevated ridge, along 20 km (12.4 miles) of winding mountain roads from the nearest town. Few accidental travellers come by this way to be inspired by its call to arms – only hunters, the occasional cross-country skiers, and those drawn by the lure of the derelict monument itself. Once, however, this was one of the most potent political icons in the Eastern Bloc.

The monument's tower was adorned with red stars three times larger than the star atop the Kremlin. It was once claimed that on a clear day, these stars could be seen from as far away as the Danube River and Romanian border in the north; and from the Greek border to the south. When it was inaugurated in 1981, the House-Monument of the Bulgarian Communist Party on Buzludzha Peak was a symbol of everything that the Bulgarian regime believed communism was, and could be.

Creating a living monument

In the late nineteenth century, Bulgaria saw a massive national revival. After almost 500 years of Ottoman rule, the April Uprising of 1876 heralded the beginning of a highly organized nationwide rebellion. The Bulgarians began to beat the Ottomans back, and the following year Tsar Alexander II of Russia led his own armies south to battle the Turks across the mountains and plains of Bulgaria – launching the Russo-Turkish War of 1877–8.

НА КРАК ПРЕЗРЕНИ
О ПАРИИ РОБИ НА Т
НА КРАК О РОБИ НА Т
ПОТИСНАТИ И УНИЖЕН
СТАВАЙТЕ СРЕЩУ ВРАГ
НЕКА БЕЗ МИЛ СТ БЕ
НЕ Р НЕМ

ЗТАРИИ
BAYERN
MÜNCHEN

02.11.2007 СЕК
BMW
ИВАНЯ
08
ТОПАНАК Б-КО
П-ЦА
17.08.03
BMW

One of the most decisive conflicts in this war was the epic Battle of Shipka Pass. This vital route across the Balkan Mountains was first captured, and then fiercely defended by 7,500 Bulgarian and Russian troops – against an onslaught by 38,000 marauding Turks from the south. It was a turning point in the country's history and the autonomous Principality of Bulgaria was established soon after.

A century later, the country was ruled by a communist regime. Much like their allies in the Soviet Union, the Bulgarian Communist Party had embraced the medium of sculpture as a means of physically expressing its Marxist-Leninist ideology; and during those years countless monuments, crafted in the larger-than-life 'socialist realist' style, would be raised throughout the country. Out of all of them though, the House-Monument of the Bulgarian Communist Party – built on Buzludzha Peak and overlooking the Shipka Pass – was by far the most extravagant.

The creation of the Buzludzha monument was to be a celebration of the 1891 birth of the Bulgarian socialist movement: an ideology literally made concrete. In so doing, the country's leaders were making a deliberate ploy to associate themselves with the nation's historic freedom-fighters.

It was also to be a working building, featuring a conference hall, meeting place and the figurative headquarters of the Bulgarian Communist Party. However, its wonderfully symbolic site did not make for an easy building location: the Buzludzha monument stands 1,441 m (4,728 ft) up a

mountain where the winter temperature can plummet to as low as -30°C and the slopes are snowbound for months of the year. It took a herculean effort from thousands of volunteers and army workers to build. The peak was first levelled using explosives, and special access roads had to be carved into the slopes of the mountain. After years of effort, it was inaugurated in 1981 in a triumphant ceremony presided over by First Secretary of the Central Committee of the Bulgarian Communist Party, Todor Zhivkov.

Scion of Socialism
In its prime, the Buzludzha monument was magnificent. It was designed by the architect Georgi Stoilov, and the tower attached to the saucer-like structure stands 107 m (351 ft) high. More than sixty Bulgarian artists worked on the elaborate murals that lined the amphitheatre and observation decks. The construction cost was in excess of 16 million Bulgarian levs (almost £7 million), a huge sum for its time.

However, less than a decade after its celebrated opening, it was deserted. In 1989, Bulgaria's communist regime toppled. The Buzludzha monument passed into the possession of a state that wanted to look forward to a democratic capitalist future, not back towards a totalitarian past. Maintaining such a remote and unfashionable monument was far from a priority. Buzludzha fell into disuse.

The power of wind and water
The monument lies 12 km (7.5 miles) up a turning off the Shipka Pass. At the top, the car park that would once have welcomed political guests has now gone to weed. A paved path snakes up to the spine of the mountain ridge, and as visitors reach the crest the spectacular monument rears up above them; its sheer size and extraordinary shape incongruous in the mountain setting.

Below the bizarre, saucer-and-spire bulk of the building itself, a long, wide flight of steps descends to a paved courtyard. Here the party faithful once gathered to listen to inspiring speeches of socialist unity. The stone stairs were flanked with mighty, sculpted flames, now reduced to weathered stumps.

The past twenty-five winters have been cruel to this once-proud building. For much of the year the Buzludzha monument is beset by heavy snow. Holes in the roof mean that drifts pile up in the auditorium. The central circular floor is often thick with ice, a virtual skating rink. Water

trickles into thin cracks in the concrete, and as it freezes it expands, so increasing the damage. Every spring the snow retreats to reveal an ever more damaged structure. Stairwells become rivers and rooms fill with fetid ponds.

Still, Buzludzha's central chamber is breathtaking. Its inspiration, according to the architect, came from the ancient Romans who built amphitheatres in the early settlements buried beneath Bulgaria's modern cities. Long low benches circle the main space. Directly above, the ceiling is proudly adorned with a colossal hammer and sickle. The fact that the roof is a ruin, crumbled in places to a rusty skeleton, only adds to the impact of this incredible place.

An array of socialist art

This was a building to honour the past and inspire the future. Its dimensions were designed to be humbling. The murals and written messages that adorn its walls were chosen with care.

The faces of communist leaders decorate the walls. A trio of iconic faces are picked out in richly coloured tiles: Engels, Marx and Lenin. Labourers, soldiers and farmers are depicted in deliberately heroic tableaux. Russian troops stride forward to Bulgaria's aid; young women welcome them with bread, salt and flowers.

Behind the prime council seats were three more portraits, with the left-most face now carefully chipped away. This was an image of Todor Zhivkov, leader of the People's Republic of Bulgaria from 1954–1989. Zhivkov served longer than any other Eastern Bloc leader, and was one of the longest ruling non-royal leaders in history. His portrait was supposedly removed at his own request – as the man

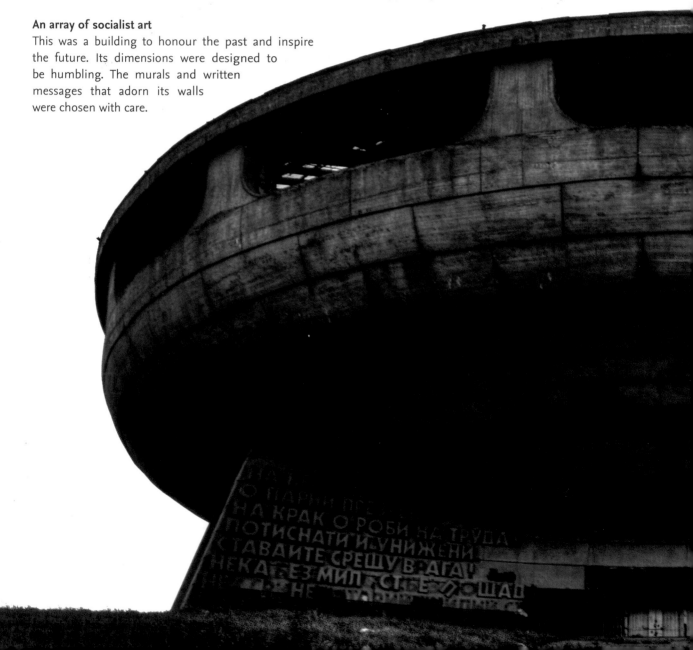

retired from public life, and attempted to distance himself from the ghosts of the crumbling regime he had once presided over.

Buzludzha's future

A piece of graffiti used to appear printed above the main entrance to the Buzludzha monument; 'FORGET YOUR PAST,' it read.

By many Bulgarians, the advice would have been well received. This nation is keen to move on from the oppression of the socialist years – and as it stands as the ultimate emblem of that ideology, to forget the saucer on Buzludzha Peak, too.

While there are also those who lament the decline of what is, undeniably, an architectural wonder, finding the support to preserve the monument is no easy thing. Of course repairs would be prohibitively expensive, but it's more than that: the monument rests in the de facto ownership of the state, but no Bulgarian politician would dare touch it for fear of being branded a 'communist' by the opposition. And so it remains – ownerless, abandoned, an orphan of history, the physical counterpart of a period that has now passed into political taboo.

However, those who would rather forget the monument altogether are in for disappointment. This hugely photogenic structure has become something of a global celebrity amongst fans of beautiful ruins, and the site today is a mecca for photographers, urban explorers and other curious travellers – many of whom travel halfway around the world to come and peer at the fading ruins of a lost socialist age. Ironically, the monument welcomes more foreign visitors now than it ever did in the days of the former regime.

EPECUÉN

Epecuén
ARGENTINA

DATE ABANDONED	TYPE OF PLACE	LOCATION	REASON	INHABITANTS	CURRENT STATUS
1985	Spa town	Argentina	Environmental	1,500 residents; 5,000 seasonal visitors	Destroyed

IT WAS A LAKESIDE HOLIDAY TOWN BLESSED WITH WARM SUMMERS AND AN IDYLLIC SETTING, UNTIL A CATASTROPHIC FLOOD WIPED IT FROM THE MAP. THEN, AFTER A QUARTER OF A CENTURY SPENT SLUMBERING IN THE DEPTHS, A DRY SPELL SAW ITS ABANDONED RUINS REVEALED.

The town that drowned

The sad irony of Villa Epecuén is this: the very waters that gave birth to the town also destroyed it. In 1920, the town was established as a spa resort beside Lago Epecuén (Lake Epecuén). This shallow lagoon is the second saltiest body of water on earth, after the Dead Sea. The therapeutic powers of its waters were touted as a cure for rheumatism, depression and skin diseases, among many other complaints. (Epecuén means 'eternal spring'.) Early visitors trekked for days to get here and soak themselves in its miraculous waters.

The country's capital, Buenos Aires, lies 550 km (340 miles) to the north and when a railway station was built nearby, Villa Epecuén was suddenly accessible as a weekend retreat. Now ordinary trippers joined those seeking a treatment. They came to stroll along the tree-lined waterfront, sit in the cafés and marvel at the wide blue skies. The spa town often drew 20,000 visitors over a season and the streets were packed with thriving business, hotels and guesthouses, luxury shops, swimming pools and promenades.

A change in the weather

Starting in the late 1970s, unusually wet weather descended on the hills around the health resort, several years in a row. For a sustained period of several weeks, prodigious amounts of rain were dumped in the catchment area around Villa Epecuén. The town sits within a vast, flat-bottomed basin and it was soon clear that the level of water in the neighbouring lagoon was rising year-on-year. At the end of May when the winter rains normally tailed off, the sky just kept pouring. The lagoon kept rising.

By 1985, Lago Epecuén was full to brimming. The town had flood protection in place, but on 6 November the salty water forced its way through a breach in a clay dam. It then overtopped the dyke that was the town's last defence. Nothing could stop the water now and the town's 1,500 residents were given the emergency order to evacuate. Villa Epecuén was drowned just hours later.

After the initial inundation the floodwater kept coming, for year after year in a creeping deluge that inched up the streets and slowly swallowed cars, trees, buildings, whole city blocks. By 1993 Villa Epecuén was totally submerged under 10 m (30 ft) of water. That's how it would stay for the next quarter of a century.

Sunk and forgotten

There was nowhere for the water to go, so the town simply sat in its giant salty puddle. Then in 2009, around twenty-five years after the rainfall had increased, the weather changed again. Several dry years in a row saw the floodwaters creep backwards across the flat plain. Like a modern-day Atlantis, Villa Epecuén was reborn from the deep.

It stands now as a ghost town in appearance as well as in nature: the heavily salted lagoon waters have coated everything in a silvery white skin. Dead trees claw at the sky like skeletal fingers. Car engines and rusty beds lie half-covered in shrouds of white. On a sunny day the buildings shine so brightly that they hurt the eyes.

The devastation here was so total that it would cost a fortune to rebuild the town. Besides, the destruction visited on the surrounding land left this a less than appealing place to come to. It's likely that the town will continue to dry out in the sun, a unique, desiccated ruin. Or perhaps the waters will come again and, unrestrained now by any dyke or dam, drown the town once more.

PRIPYAT

Pripyat

UKRAINE

DATE ABANDONED	TYPE OF PLACE	LOCATION	REASON	INHABITANTS	CURRENT STATUS
1986	New town	Chernobyl, Ukraine	Nuclear accident	49,400	Under observation

PRIPYAT WAS A MARVEL OF COMMUNIST SOCIAL PLANNING: A PLANNED TOWN OF LEAFY AVENUES AND FIRST-CLASS AMENITIES THAT NEARLY 50,000 PEOPLE CALLED HOME. INHABITED FOR ONLY SIXTEEN YEARS, IT WAS COMPLETELY EVACUATED IN APRIL 1986 WHEN THE WORST NUCLEAR DISASTER IN HISTORY UNFOLDED JUST THREE KILOMETRES AWAY.

The second the clocks stopped in Ukraine

The sun usually sets slowly on abandoned societies. There is certainly a turning point, but the decline and fall take place over months, years or even decades. Pripyat's demise can be timed to the second, however: life here effectively ended at 1.23:40 a.m. on 26 April 1986. That's when Reactor 4 at Chernobyl's nuclear power station blew its top and set off the worst nuclear accident in history.

Pripyat was founded in 1970 at the same time as construction began on the Chernobyl Nuclear Power Plant. It was to be a model socialist city, primarily for the families of workers at the model Soviet generating station just 3 km (1.9 miles) away. The broad, tree-lined streets had an abundance of facilities: fifteen primary schools and five secondary schools for the town's 5,000 children, a cultural complex (the 'Palace of Culture') with cinema and school of arts. Pripyat had two sports stadiums, three swimming pools, several gyms and its own hospital; as well as dozens of shops, restaurants, bars and cafés.

Reactor 1 began generating electricity in 1977, and by 1983 there were four reactors operating – each producing 1,000 megawatts (MW) of electricity. The plant delivered 10 per cent of Ukraine's total electricity by this stage. In April 1986 two further reactors were under construction, but they would never be completed.

The accident

The explosion was caused by a perfect storm of human mistakes, poor training and flawed reactor design. Ironically, this storm had its origin in a safety test. Engineers wanted to be sure that a reactor could keep running even if external power was lost. The test plan was to simulate the loss of external power and then use the steam turbine's power to keep the coolant running until the slow-starting diesel backup generators could kick in and take over the pumping. This meant running the nuclear reactor down to a low power level – engineers then turned off the automatic fail-safe mechanisms in order to allow the test to proceed, instead relying on manual safety controls. They then lowered the control rods into the core. This caused a power spike – not necessarily a problem – only now the system couldn't shut itself down. Within three seconds the power output surged from 530 MW to 33,000 MW. A colossal steam explosion sheared

Deserted apartment blocks in the town that 50,000 people once called home.

In the foreground, a monument to the victims; in the background, the blown reactor lies inside its sarcophagus.

The 'Elephant's Foot' ten years after the disaster. Although only emitting one-tenth of the radiation it once had, only 500 seconds of exposure would still prove fatal.

off the 2,000 tonne upper plate of the reactor and blew it through the roof. A second, larger explosion blew the core to bits, showering the area with highly radioactive material, which then caught fire.

Fuelling the fire
The flat roofs of the reactor building and turbine hall had been waterproofed with bitumen – contrary to safety regulations. When superheated lumps of flaming graphite landed on the bitumen it caught fire. Firefighters were on the scene quickly, but they hadn't been briefed that this was a fire from a reactor meltdown. They assumed it was a more routine electrical fire and wore very little protection. Many of them kicked the radioactive lumps of graphite and even handled them. Some unprotected workers received fatal doses of radiation in less than a minute. The reactor fire was finally extinguished on 10 May, after 5,000 tonnes of sand, lead, clay and neutron-absorbing boron had been dropped on it by helicopters.

The evacuation
The accident wasn't mentioned by Soviet state media for two days. Classical music was played on the radio instead of news. The outside world didn't know there was a major problem until scientists at a nuclear plant in Sweden, 1,000 km (620 miles) away, pointed out that their radiation readings were through the roof. Even after an announce-ment was made, it was claimed that damage was minimal and any evacuations would only be for a matter of days.

The people of Pripyat weren't evacuated until 36 hours after the incident, even though some people began coughing and vomiting just hours after the explosion. Scores of people were soon reporting severe headaches and a metallic taste in their mouths. Two people died at the scene of the explosion, four died when a firefighting helicopter crashed and thirty-two more died of acute radiation sickness soon after. Some 135,000 people were evacuated from the area, including 50,000 from Pripyat.

There were also significant long-term effects over a wide area in subsequent years. These included unusual patterns of cancer occurring from Belarus in the north down to Bulgaria in the south. The International Atomic Energy Agency has estimated that the eventual causal death toll may be 4,000. The most heavily contaminated areas were in Ukraine, Belarus, and Russia, and at least 350,400 people were evacuated in these countries. The radioactive cloud drifted much further, though: sheep in northern England and reindeer in Lapland had to be destroyed as they had been irradiated. Overall, more than seven million people were affected in some way by the fallout.

Cleaning up the mess
The final radiation breach from Chernobyl was equivalent to 400 Hiroshimas. The authorities eventually established a quarantine area 30 km (18 miles) in diameter around the reactor – the 'Zone of Alienation'.

To protect the other reactors and contain any further radioactive emissions, the whole of Reactor 4 was capped with a vast concrete sarcophagus. It was the largest civil engineering task in history; more than 250,000 construction workers were involved, and all received their permitted lifetime limits of radiation.

Today, deep inside Reactor 4 lurks one of the most extraordinary, and most lethal, objects on earth: the 'Elephant's Foot'. This is a lump of 'corium' – a blend of reactor core, nuclear fuel, fission products, control rods and concrete from the reactor room floor that melted together into a lava-like mixture then subsequently set. Although only 2 m (6.6 ft) wide, it weighs hundreds of tonnes and is so radioactive it could kill a person within minutes.

The three other reactors at the Chernobyl plant ran for several more years; the last of these was finally turned off in December 2000.

Pripyat, the dark tourist Mecca

The town of Pripyat was completely off-limits to everyone except scientists and workers until 2002, but is now open for organized tours. Thousands of people now visit to capture some of the most evocative images of abandonment that any place could offer.

The derelict Ferris wheel is one of the most iconic of all Pripyat's landmarks. It stands in the town's amusement park, which was not open at the time of the disaster – it had only just been built and was scheduled for a grand opening on May Day, 1986. The only time the park was ever used was the day after the accident, 27 April, when the authorities opened it for a few hours to distract people just before the evacuation was announced. Decorations for the opening gala still adorn the decaying rides today.

Walking round Pripyat is fascinating, and at times deeply moving. In a few homes, tables are still set for dinner and clothes still hang in wardrobes, forgotten in the swift exodus. However, most of the apartments have been ransacked – either by their fleeing occupants, or by subsequent looters – and nature has taken over what humans left behind. Young trees burst through tiled floors; vines twist their way round the metal frames of the fairground rides; apple trees hang low with fruit in autumn – though little of it will be eaten.

The effect of radiation during a day trip is calculated as being negligible: in the region of a few microsieverts per hour, compared with a fatal dose of 3–5 million microsieverts. However, staff still have to be careful how many tours they run, and how long they spend in the area near the reactors in particular. Radiation levels at the power plant will be completely back to normal in the year AD 22,000, or thereabouts.

CENTRALIA

Centralia
**UNITED STATES
OF AMERICA**

DATE ABANDONED	TYPE OF PLACE	LOCATION	REASON	INHABITANTS	CURRENT STATUS
1980s	Town	Pennsylvania	Underground fire	1,400	9 inhabitants

IN 1962, A COAL SEAM CAUGHT FIRE BENEATH CENTRALIA AND ALL EFFORTS TO EXTINGUISH IT FAILED. AS LETHAL FUMES SPEWED INTO THE AIR, THE INHABITANTS MOVED OUT – ALL EXCEPT A FEW WHO WOULD RATHER DIE IN THE TOWN THEY LOVED, HOWEVER TOXIC IT MAY BE, THAN MOVE TO PASTURES NEW.

The town with the burning streets

There's no need for a road sign telling drivers on Pennsylvania Route 61 that they're approaching Centralia – at the city limits the tarmac is buckled and rent into great smoking fissures. In Manhattan, the streets steam because of venting from the hot water pipes that run underground. Here, it's because the very earth is on fire.

Beneath the remains of this Pennsylvania coal town is a subterranean inferno that covers 1.6 km² (400 acres) and is expanding on four fronts. The fire has been burning for fifty years, and has fuel enough to burn for 250 more.

A town built on coal

The first miners came to Centralia in 1856, and soon there was a new pit opening virtually every year. By 1890, the town was flourishing: it had 2,761 residents, seven churches, five hotels, twenty-seven saloons, two theatres, a bank, a post office and over a dozen shops.

Coal production peaked in the late 1920s; after that, the stock market crash of 1929 led to the closure of five Centralia mines. However, production continued at several deep pits, as well as many strip and opencast mines, and

there was still plenty of coal being dug out of the ground in 1962. Then disaster struck.

No smoke without fire

Ironically, it's likely that the fire was started by firefighters. In May 1962, the local council asked the fire department to clean up the town's landfill facility. Their customary method of doing this was to set the refuse alight, damping the flames down when the job was done. However, the landfill site was actually an old strip mine, and the flames found their way down a seam and into the labyrinthine caverns in the coal beneath Centralia. Fire teams tried to stop the spread of the fire by collapsing many of the abandoned pits nearby, but the conflagration had too strong a hold and all efforts to stop it failed.

At first, the decline was slow. Twenty years after the fire had started the town's population had shrunk from around 1,400 to just over 1,000.

Then, in 1981, the earth started to swallow people. Centralia made national headlines when a 46 m (150 ft) deep sinkhole suddenly opened up beneath a 12-year-old boy in his own backyard. Luckily the boy's cousin managed to pull him out before the ground fell completely

away. However, the scalding hot gases that vented from the hole were analysed and found to contain a lethal level of carbon monoxide.

Around the same time, a gas-station owner had noticed that his underground fuel tanks seemed warm. He lowered a thermometer into a gasoline tank – the fuel was at 77.8°C (172°F). The mass exodus of Centralia began in earnest.

The US Government offered financial aid for people to move away, but a few hold-out families stayed on. When people did move away, their properties were bulldozed. Throughout the 1980s the noxious emissions increased, the sinkholes grew in size and frequency and the fractures crept ever-outward along the highways. In 1992, the town was officially condemned and ten years later Centralia was removed from maps when the United States Postal Service revoked its ZIP code.

Life is snuffed out

Seen from a nearby ridge, Centralia today looks like a low-lying field with a few roads running through it – as if a small airport had been reclaimed by nature. The few homes that still stand today are several blocks apart and their sides have been shored up with buttresses to stop them falling down. It's hard to imagine that not long ago this area was covered with block after block of housing. Kids bicycled along the pavements and played in the gardens, and vehicles trundled down the smooth roads.

The lone church, St Mary's, appears boarded up and derelict yet still opens for prayer every Sunday. The hellish fires below seem not to have dared touch its foundations. The town's four cemeteries are also in good condition, although one that lies on the crest of a hill has wraiths of smoke rising out of it. This is said to be the inspiration for the notoriously spooky video game *Silent Hill*.

There are officially nine people living here amid the smoking rubble, but it's only a matter of time before Centralia has a population of zero. Then, but for the hissing of poisonous gas and the slow cracking of the earth, the toxic ghost town will be finally silent.

TOP LEFT: St Mary's Church
BOTTOM LEFT: Houses have lost their neighbours, and stand on unsteady foundations.

YOUNG PIONEER CAMP

DATE ABANDONED	TYPE OF PLACE	LOCATION	REASON	INHABITANTS	CURRENT STATUS
1980s	Youth camp	Near Moscow	Political	Hundreds visiting at any one time	Abandoned

THIS BIZARRE CAMP IN THE RUSSIAN WOODS WAS DESIGNED TO ENTERTAIN, HOUSE AND INDOCTRINATE CHILDREN IN THE IDEALS OF COMMUNIST LIFE. IT WAS ONE OF THOUSANDS OF SUCH INSTITUTIONS THAT NOW STAND ABANDONED – YET SURELY NOT FORGOTTEN BY THE YOUNGSTERS WHO WENT THERE.

Scouts of the Soviet Union

The pine forests north of Moscow extend for mile after green mile, a seeming wilderness that is only occasionally broken by straight, featureless highways. Few passing motorists could have imagined however, the bizarre place that lies hidden deep in the heart of the woods; for here is a forgotten Soviet holiday camp for children, frightening in its austerity, and apparently designed by a Russian admirer of surrealist Salvador Dali. Welcome to the Young Pioneer Camp.

Young Pioneers of communism

The first state-governed Young Pioneer holiday park was built in Ukraine in 1925 and was immediately popular. It was an adaptation of the Scout camp concept, which had been established in Russia before the Revolution of 1917. Many changes were superficial: the Scout motto of 'Be prepared!' was adapted to 'Always prepared!' Just as at Scout camps, the children played sports and learned outdoor skills and self-reliance. Many camps also gave youngsters career-specific education in engineering, geology and biology. The startling animal sculptures at the camp shown here are perhaps evidence that this one was aimed at future naturalists. Fundamentally, however, the Scout Movement was re-engineered to suit the goals of a communist society.

The pioneer camps were very much a state propaganda tool first, and an adventure centre second. The primary goal of Lenin's Young Pioneer Organisation was to sow the seeds of communist ideals into fertile young minds. The imagery and daily routines were carefully planned to inculcate the Soviet ideology. Children wore a uniform with red neck scarf, carried red banners and flags, and sported a badge with a picture of Lenin on it. They also had to swear an oath to Lenin when they joined:

Every year millions of Soviet
children spent part of their school
holidays at one of the country's
40,000 Young Pioneer camps.

Solemn promise of a pioneer of the Soviet Union

'I (surname, given name), having now joined the ranks of the Vladimir Illyich Lenin All-Union Pioneer Organization, in the presence of my comrades solemnly promise: to passionately love my fatherland and to cherish it as I can, to live, study, and fight as the Great Lenin has instructed, as the Communist Party teaches me, and to always carry out the laws of the Pioneers of the Soviet Union.'

The movement became a growing phenomenon and more camps were built. From Poland and Belarus in the west they stretched all the way to China and North Korea in the east. Many of the camps in North Korea are still active today. At least 10 million children holidayed in the USSR's 40,000 pioneer camps during the 1960s and 1970s.

The camps were used for exchange visits of children from different communist countries. A few Western children even holidayed here, their trips arranged by groups that promoted international understanding, or by parents who had been born east of the Iron Curtain.

ABOVE: The animal sculptures suggest this was probably a camp for children interested in nature.

TOP: The extraordinary architecture was presumably intended to inspire, rather than terrify, young people.

The fun starts here

The camps were usually in remote locations: in the middle of a forest; a valley amid high mountains, beside an isolated lake. Here the children could enjoy all that nature had to offer, while being watched by father Lenin – a statue of the great leader often stood at the camp's centre.

Mornings started with a bugle reveille. The children scrambled into their gym clothes for a rousing exercise session before breakfast. Then they changed into their formal camp uniforms ready for morning assembly. Every day a different young pioneer was honoured by being chosen to raise the red flag as the Russian national anthem was played.

Some camps took the children on excursions. These could be to swimming pools, a war memorial or to meet a high-up government official. If they were very lucky they might get to visit a state-run farm and be given an informative talk about milk quotas, but there was also plenty of time for relaxing and making friends. There were campfires, walks in the woods, art, drama, music and highly competitive games of chess.

The holidays are over

This particular camp was abandoned in the mid 1980s, one of many that fell into disuse as the former USSR crumbled politically. The Young Pioneers formally broke up in 1991. Since then, some camps have been repurposed into youth centres with a less totalitarian take on summer activities. There still must be dozens, if not hundreds, however, that are now simply rotting away in far-flung corners of the vast Soviet empire. These camps must have made such a strong impression on Russian children that they will surely be remembered for a long time – either with fondness or, in the case of this one with its ghastly deep sea creatures and carnivorous decor, perhaps dread.

TOP: The camps were designed to encourage patriotism and belief in Soviet ideals.

JURAGUA

Juragua○ CUBA

DATE ABANDONED	TYPE OF PLACE	LOCATION	REASON	INHABITANTS	CURRENT STATUS
1992	Nuclear power station	Cuba	Economic	Dozens of workers	Unfinished

POKING ABOVE THE CUBAN TREETOPS ARE THE CONCRETE STUMPS OF AN ATOMIC DREAM. FROM HERE WAS TO FLOW LIMITLESS POWER TO FUEL THE MODEL COMMUNIST SOCIETY. NOW IT WILL NEVER BE FINISHED, AS THE ISLAND LEAVES ITS SOVIET ERA FURTHER AND FURTHER BEHIND.

Island with an energy crisis

The 1959 Cuban Revolution blew away the rampant corruption of the previous regime, and the new communist government set out to make landmark social and economic advances. Energy production, however, was not to be one of its success stories. The island state has always been dependent on imported oil, which bleeds the country of what little hard currency it has. Cuba also had severe problems with its conventional power stations; inefficient and out-dated, these often operated far below their design outputs leading to frequent blackouts. Nuclear power promised to release Cuba from the shackles of foreign oil companies and solve its electricity-generating crisis. The country looked around for a partner to help it enter the atomic age.

Swapping partners

Ironically, Cuba's first steps into nuclear power were taken with the US. In 1956 the two countries signed an 'Agreement for Co-Operation Concerning Civil Uses of Atomic Energy'. This laid the foundations for Cuba to design, build and operate a nuclear power station with US expertise. The Cuba signatory on this document was the US's pocket-dictator Fulgencio Batista; three years later he was ousted in the Cuban Revolution. Fidel Castro was now prime minister of a communist state, and highly distrustful of the North Americans. By the time of the Cuban Missile Crisis in 1962, the US–Cuban nuclear agreement was history.

The Russians were more than happy to take over as Cuba's nuclear partners however, and in 1967 they agreed to help Cuba build a research reactor for experimental and teaching purposes. By 1976 the two countries had outlined a deal to build no less than twelve nuclear reactors at four sites. Ultimately, this plan was downgraded to just two 440-megawatt reactors at Juragua. However, the reactors were the latest Soviet design and Juragua's first reactor alone would have supplied over 15 per cent of Cuba's energy needs.

The Soviet Union flew in 450 experienced nuclear technicians and work on the first reactor began in 1983, with a predicted completion date of 1993. Initially the build went well, and construction of a second reactor began in 1985.

America's nuclear neighbour

The US's already-frosty attitude towards Cuba wasn't warmed by the prospect of a Russian-built nuclear reactor just 290 km (180 miles) off its Florida doorstep. When the Soviet reactor at Chernobyl, in Ukraine, exploded in 1986 in the world's worst-ever nuclear accident, the relationship became positively frigid.

Meanwhile, construction was not going as smoothly as had been hoped. Soviet subsidies were reduced, then removed. The declining Cuban economy caused further delays. The collapse of the Soviet Union in 1991 threw an almighty spanner in the works at Juragua; the fragmenting communist empire was no longer prepared to just hand Cuba money and resources. Construction was suspended in 1992 and most of the Russian technicians were recalled home. Although construction of the first building was nearly complete, inside only 37 per cent of the reactor equipment had been installed. The second reactor was only 20–30 per cent complete. None of the primary components in either reactor had been installed, and no nuclear fuel had been delivered.

Furthermore, there were huge problems with what had been built so far: a senior Cuban scientist who had worked in quality control at Juragua, and later defected, reported that 60 per cent of the Soviet material shipped for the two reactors was defective.

There were attempts to resume construction in 1995, but these came to nothing. Since then several investors have expressed interest, but the US is still not at all happy at the idea of these archaic, crumbling reactors being completed. In 2000, Vladimir Putin flirted with the idea of helping Castro finish the plant, but this initiative has also stalled.

Awaiting the big switch on

The dangerous site is still guarded and visitors are not allowed. The few people who have glimpsed inside report a huge and empty turbine hall, twelve storeys tall, surrounded by a warren of dark, concrete rooms where technicians and scientists were supposed to have worked. Lattices of steel beams stand unclad and black holes in the floor drop away to mysterious depths. It is an ideal home for bats, and other nocturnal jungle creatures.

The reactors were built close to the ocean, so that seawater could be used as a coolant. Now the canals, pipes and culverts connecting the plant to the Caribbean Sea are rank with vegetation and swarming with mosquitoes.

A few kilometres from the nuclear plant is Ciudad Nuclear, Cuba's version of Pripyat in Ukraine. This was designed as an idyllic model town with broad boulevards and open spaces around the houses. However, most buildings were unfinished and now stand as empty concrete shells. The few structures that were completed look dated and uncared for. The skeleton apartment blocks are a stark reminder of the failure of an international communist dream.

TOP RIGHT: The Juragua nuclear plant under construction in 1988.

BOTTOM RIGHT: The plant was built close to the sea to ensure a supply of water.

ROSARIO ISLAND VILLAS

Rosario Islands

COLOMBIA

DATE ABANDONED	TYPE OF PLACE	LOCATION	REASON	INHABITANTS	CURRENT STATUS
1993	Private residence	Colombia	Owner's death	Dozens	Derelict

IT WAS THE ISLAND HOLIDAY HOME OF ONE OF THE RICHEST MEN ON THE PLANET – WHO ALSO HAPPENED TO BE A MOST NOTORIOUS CRIMINAL. FROM HERE PABLO ESCOBAR CONTROLLED A SMUGGLING EMPIRE THAT SHIPPED HUNDREDS OF TONNES OF COCAINE, MURDERED THOUSANDS OF PEOPLE AND EARNED HIM UNCOUNTABLE BILLIONS OF DOLLARS.

Mountains of money

Pablo Escobar was the street thief who became the wealthiest criminal in history. In the 1980s he rapidly graduated from hustling cigarettes and fake lottery tickets in the suburbs of Medellín to smuggling 15 tonnes of cocaine a day into the United States.

The 'King of Cocaine' became the wealthiest criminal in history, with a fortune of around US$30 billion by the early 1990s. Most of this was held as cash, and every week Escobar reportedly spent $1,000 just on rubber bands to wrap the $420 million that the cartel would earn in that time.

The money was stacked in huge warehouses where rats ate their way through millions in hundred dollar bills; but at these stakes, a loss of 10 per cent to the rodents was considered acceptable 'spoilage'. In 1992 alone, the rats scoffed a share of around $1 billion (£600 million).

Playground of the players

One of the fruits of Escobar's illicit labour was this now-crumbling villa on the Rosario Islands. These beautiful tropical isles lie off Colombia's Caribbean coast, 32 km (20 miles) from Cartagena, and they were the holiday hangouts of choice for many of the country's rich and notorious in the 1980s and 1990s.

Escobar and his fellow drug lords ruled the waves here, having paid off the police and any coastguard who might prowl these waters. They were free to build opulent mansions in beautifully landscaped gardens with fountains and swimming pools. Escobar's villa complex was by far the biggest, with its own private nightclub, beautifully tiled

pool, cool terraces and shady palm trees. One building was constructed from coral bricks chiselled out of nearby reefs – the protected marine ecosystem didn't mean much to a man who dealt in death every day.

This was a glamorous playground for those in the master smuggler's inner circle. Here, some of the most powerful men in South America could talk business, party and store more money than they could ever hope to spend.

The cost of his success

The booming cocaine trade helped turn Colombia into the world's most murderous country: there were 27,100 violent deaths in 1992, and Escobar's own hitmen were responsible for the murders of over 600 policemen.

In 1993, Escobar's life ended just as it had been lived: violently. The increasingly infuriated Colombian and US governments put a Special Forces-trained police task force

on his trail. The smuggler was tracked, then shot and killed while fleeing across a rooftop.

Escobar had cultivated a 'Robin Hood' image in the poorer districts of Colombia, where he paid for the construction of hospitals, schools and sports centres. He sponsored children's football teams and even built several churches. In death he remained popular among the poor: 25,000 people attended his funeral.

Decay in paradise

The villas and beach houses that once belonged to Escobar and his confederates are now owned by the Colombian Government. Until the state decides exactly what to do with these once ill-gotten gains, nature is now the boss here.

The tropical heat and salty air have taken their toll on the whitewashed walls and cool tiles. The wooden lookout house where Escobar's guards scanned the seas for police boats is now a rundown and ramshackle ruin. The elegant rooms around the swimming pool are full of dust and insects.

Where Escobar's fleet of seaplanes stuffed with drugs and money once came in to land on the turquoise waters, now tourists on jet skis and pleasure boats zip around.

Despite the decay, it's easy to imagine the scenes that must have played out here; how the next round of smuggling schemes, bribes and murders would all have been discussed over drinks beside the sun-dappled swimming pool. Now the pool is puddled with brackish rainwater and the tiles are cracking. The fall of the greatest drugs empire the world has ever seen was just as swift and sure as its rise had been.

TOP LEFT: This villa is made of rare coral chiselled from the seabed.
TOP RIGHT: Millionaire cartel members once partied round this poolside.

LONDON UNDERGROUND STATIONS

UNITED KINGDOM

London Underground Stations

DATE ABANDONED	TYPE OF PLACE	LOCATION	REASON	INHABITANTS	CURRENT STATUS
Various	Underground railway stations	London	Economic	0	Disused/Preserved as film sets

DEEP BENEATH THE CITY, JUST FEET FROM THE HURRYING COMMUTERS, LIES A HIDDEN WORLD OF GHOST STATIONS. MANY ARE ONLY PLATFORMS, HALF-GLIMPSED IN THE SHADOWY TUNNELS BUT SOME ARE PERFECTLY PRESERVED, WAITING FOR PASSENGERS WHO WILL NEVER COME.

The end of the line

Holborn Station is where the fourth busiest Tube line, the Piccadilly, interchanges with the busiest, the Central line. Travellers here might notice another platform though, locked off behind a grilled door but well lit and with advertising billboards plastered to its curving wall. The rails are clear and it looks as if a train could arrive at any second. But the next connection will be a long wait, as no passenger train has run here since 1994.

Going underground – for a little way

Aldwych Station opened in 1907 with the name 'Strand', after the street beneath which it is located. This name can still be seen on the facade today. It was the terminus – and only station – on a side branch of the Piccadilly line that was originally meant to run much further. The original plan involving the Aldwych branch was for a tube line that would run from Wood Green southwards through King's Cross to Strand, then on to meet the Metropolitan line at Temple. However, the Duke of Norfolk, who owned the land north of Temple, objected. It ended as a poor compromise; a line to nowhere. The stub seemed doubly pointless as it only had one station, and because that station was so close to Holborn it was usually quicker to walk to one's destination.

However, it was opened with optimism: the line had regular services running through from the Piccadilly line, while a special train ran in the evenings for theatregoers heading to the Strand area.

The station was closed during the Second World War and its platforms and tunnels were used as bomb shelters for artworks from London's public galleries and museums, including the Elgin Marbles. It reopened after the war but

The facade of Aldwych Underground Station in 2012, eighteen years after the last passenger service was withdrawn.

PICCADILLY RLY
STRAND STATION
STRAND WC2
THIS SIDE
← 234-170
169-1 →
OTHER SIDE
← 235-265
AND
AUSTRALIA
HOUSE
BUSH HOUSE →
AND
336-460
CITY OF WESTMINSTER
RVP
Fire exit
Keep clear
Fire exit
Keep clear

was always one of the less-used stations on the network. By 1993 only 450 passengers a day were boarding its trains and it was losing £150,000 per year. It closed the year after.

Passengers heading east on the Piccadilly line can still glimpse the old tunnel branch on their right hand side just after leaving Holborn station. Part of the remaining platform at Holborn is kept in use today and is a practice ground for new signage and advertising displays.

Aldwych has turned its authentic appearance and central location into a filmmaking resource. It is unique among mothballed stations in that it is kept in operational condition, with a train permanently parked on the branch. This can be driven up and down the branch for filming.

In 2015, Aldwych station was proposed as a gateway to a new network of subterranean cycle paths, utilizing disused London Underground tunnels. Perhaps commuters will once more pass along its deserted platforms.

Stations in the shadows

Aldwych might be the best-known of the disused stations on the London Underground system, but there are dozens of others. Some were closed for economic reasons, others were half built but then never completed. A few were bypassed altogether when alternative routes were bored through the clay beneath the city.

The remains of several are still visible above ground: a shop front is framed by an arch of glossy red tiles; a curiously shaped ventilation shaft that stands alone at a traffic junction; old red bricks just visible under the ever-changing graffiti. Other stations have been wiped clean from the city's surface, but retain a ghostly presence underground: dark and dusty platforms that suddenly appear out of the blackness between regular stations; trackless tunnel branches curving off to who-knows-where; locked doors hiding stairways no longer hiked up by commuters.

There are also many functioning stations with secretive sides that they keep hidden away. There are blocked off passageways at Euston station with 1969 film posters still pasted on the walls – there's an unused ticket hall too, beautifully decorated in cream and green tiles, and furnished with wooden telephone booths from the 1930s, walled off in their alcove rather than modernized.

PLYMOUTH

DATE ABANDONED	TYPE OF PLACE	LOCATION	REASON	INHABITANTS	CURRENT STATUS
1995	Island capital	Montserrat, West Indies	Volcanic eruption	4,000	Buried under ash

FOR THREE CENTURIES THIS WHITEWASHED COLONIAL TOWN HAD BEEN THE HUB OF LIFE ON THE LUSH TROPICAL ISLAND. THEN, IN JUST ONE CATACLYSMIC SUMMER, HALF OF THE TINY NATION WAS BURIED IN RED-HOT VOLCANIC ASH – AND THE JEWEL OF MONTSERRAT WAS DULLED FOREVER.

MONTSERRAT
(UK)
○ Plymouth

ABOVE: Plymouth's Courthouse building buried in lahar deposits from the Soufrière Hills volcano.

OVERLEAF:
The volcano deposits yet more ash on the town.

The emerald of the Empire

Plymouth was the capital of Montserrat, a teardrop-shaped island about the size of Jersey that is part of a chain of islands called the Lesser Antilles. The island has been a British overseas territory since 1632, and the characteristic touch of the motherland was evident in the Georgian colonial homes and red telephone boxes.

The island's rugged coastline and lush green hills, and the presence of many residents of Irish descent, earned it the soubriquet, 'The Emerald Isle of the Caribbean'. (God Save The Queen may be the national anthem, but St Patrick's Day is a major celebration on the island.)

In 1995 it would get a new nickname: 'The Pompeii of the Caribbean'. Its tropical forests, sparkling waterfalls and thriving capital city would be drowned forever in deadly rivers of ash.

Glamour beneath the palms

Montserrat was everything one imagines a Caribbean island to be. Christopher Columbus was the first European to admire it, when he stopped by on 11 November 1493 and gave the island its name – which means 'jagged mountain'.

At the heart of the island are the Soufrière Hills, a favoured picnic spot where the splashes of waterfalls echoed through the mango trees. In the elegant streets of Plymouth, the dreamy beats of calypso music pulsed through the warm air. In the cafés the diners tucked into the local speciality of mountain chicken – in reality the giant ditch frog – washed down with rum punches.

In 1977 The Beatles' producer, Sir George Martin, established AIR Studios here: a recording facility as advanced as any in London, but set in a considerably more exotic location. For more than a decade, AIR Montserrat was where rock's crème de la crème came to lay down their latest albums. Dire Straits, The Police, Sir Paul McCartney, Sir Elton John, Michael Jackson, Stevie Wonder, The Rolling Stones and Eric Clapton all made music in this tropical hideaway. Glamorous stars could often be seen sipping cold Carib beers at cafés in town after a recording session.

Perhaps the only clue to the island's latent, savage, nature was its black sand beaches; for black sand is created, often instantaneously, when lava hits seawater and fragments as it rapidly cools.

Live by the sword, die by the sword

It's only thanks to volcanic activity that Montserrat exists at all. Lava bubbled up from a vent in the seabed twenty-five million years ago, broached the surface and finally congealed into the island we see today.

There were minor earthquakes in the 1900s and 1930s, but these tremors didn't develop into any significant volcanic activity. There had been no notable eruptions since the nineteenth century. The volcano, however, was about to make up for lost time.

In 1992 the beast within the mountain began to growl – and a series of earthquakes rocked the island. Then in July 1995, 502 years after Christopher Columbus passed by, the beast *roared*. Magma rising within the Soufrière Hills volcano heated groundwater causing it to evaporate nearly instantaneously. This caused a catastrophic explosion of steam, water, ash and rock. Plymouth, 6 km (3.7 miles) away was suffocated by a thick shroud of ash that turned day into night. Clouds of ash plumed up to 12,000 m (40,000 feet) into the atmosphere.

Two thirds of the island was covered in ash. Plymouth was evacuated in December and became a ghost town. For over a year there were regular explosive eruptions and pyroclastic flows – rivers of super-heated gas and molten rock that suddenly burst from the volcano and surged down the slopes at terrifying speeds, instantly killing any and all living things in their path. These unstoppable walls of death carry vast amounts of dust and ash, which are deposited like sediment when the flow stops.

In August 1997, the volcano became even more violent, spewing magma in the most intense series of eruptions to date. Pyroclastic flows flooded the already ruined Plymouth with 12 m (39 ft) of mud and ash, turning it into a modern-day Pompeii. In many places only the rooftops are still visible – elsewhere, the buildings have been completely swallowed. Nineteen farm workers were killed by these eruptions.

By now the whole southern half of the island was rendered uninhabitable. The island's airport was smeared into oblivion by a pyroclastic flow.

A capital city obliterated

For a larger country, such destruction would have been a serious wound. However, alternatives would be found relatively quickly and there would be a recovery. For Montserrat this was a decapitation: Plymouth was the capital and largest town with 4,000 residents, nearly all the rural island's shops and services, and the seat of government too. Three and a half centuries of civilization was drowned in a sea of mud, almost overnight.

Two-thirds of the island's population, 7,000 people, simply left. Many of them were shipped out on the British destroyer HMS *Liverpool*. At least 4,000 travelled to the United Kingdom; some fled to other islands nearby, such as Antigua and Barbuda. Most who departed have not returned.

Exploring today

Montserrat is an island of two halves. There is lush green vegetation in the north, with houses, schools and a reviving tourist industry. The south is a wasteland, an ash-covered dead zone.

The hillside village of Brades is home to new government buildings, schools, a bank, police and fire stations, making it the island's de facto capital. In 2005 a new airport opened, perched on an airy shelf of land in the northern part of the island. A quarter of the island's 4,800 remaining residents turned out to cheer the first tiny plane in to land.

Plymouth is well and truly abandoned. It does, however, draw lots of visitors. The Soufrière Hills volcano is one of the world's finest natural laboratories for volcanologists. Some permanent scientists and many visiting ones bring much needed money into the devastated island. A live volcano is also quite an attraction for passing cruise ships, which ease as near as they dare to the smoking monster.

The island is, geographically at least, growing. The Montserrat Volcano Observatory reports that the 15 m (49 ft) thick pyroclastic flows that have reached the sea at Trant's Bay have extended the island's coastline up to 650 m (2,100 ft) further out into the ocean.

HOTEL DEL SALTO

DATE ABANDONED	TYPE OF PLACE	LOCATION	REASON	INHABITANTS	CURRENT STATUS
1990s	Hotel	Near Bogotá, Colombia	Economic	Hotel guests and staff	Abandoned/ Museum

Hotel del Salto
COLOMBIA

THE HOTEL DEL SALTO WAS WHERE THE WEALTHY SOCIALITES OF COLOMBIA'S CAPITAL CITY CAME TO GET AWAY FROM IT ALL. THEY HAD AN UNBEATABLE VIEW OF ONE OF THE COUNTRY'S MOST SPECTACULAR NATURAL ATTRACTIONS, BUT THE GLORY DAYS OF THIS UNIQUE GETAWAY DID NOT LAST LONG.

Crumbling on a clifftop

The hotel's roof is tiled with decades of moss. Neat rows of seedlings sprout in the gutters, full-grown trees flourish on the terrace and the blank windows are coated in damp algal grime. From a distance the building seems to be growing from the sheer cliff face, but up close its grip looks more uncertain. The hotel teeters on the edge of a misty abyss, as if ready to throw itself to a watery doom in the cascade that crashes onto the rocks far below.

This is the Hotel del Salto, which stands overlooking the Tequendama Falls in Colombia. The image of a fate-oppressed building is fitting, for the locals will happily spin tales of its haunting by the ghosts of forbidden lovers – who checked in and then threw themselves off the craggy cataract beyond.

Rooms with a view

At Tequendama the Bogotá River plummets 132 m (433 ft) into a gorge. The falls vary from being totally dry in December to thundering and apocalyptic in spring. They pour into an arena formed from spectacular cliffs of pinkish stratified rock topped with lush vegetation. When the wet season swells the river into a charging torrent its plunge over the lip of the falls creates a thick bowl of mist. The mossy stones, flaking plaster and empty black eyes of the hotel look particularly foreboding in these conditions.

The hotel was built in 1924 to capitalize on this unique vista. The wealthy members of Bogotá society would journey the 30 km (19 miles) by train to enjoy the finest food and drink amid unparalleled scenery. The place was a success at first and expansion plans were tabled in 1950 that would have seen the hotel soar to eighteen storeys. However, these fell through and the hotel then fell from grace, limping on through the next few decades with only five of its fifteen rooms in regular use.

Furthermore, although the river beyond is picturesque, it is also filthy. Raw effluent from the six million citizens of Bogotá is dumped straight into the river just south of the city, making it a virtual sewer. By the 1990s the river environment around the hotel was far from pleasant and the building was abandoned. It remained deserted in the jungle mists for two decades.

Rebirth as a museum

The falls are a major tourist attraction and the ruined building on the edge of a misty gulf has been a favourite sight of visitors here. Part of the hotel has recently been refurbished as a museum by the National University of Colombia; but when the river thunders and the mists rise, it still looks as lost and lonely as it ever did.

BEELITZ SANATORIUM

Beelitz
Sanatorium

GERMANY

DATE ABANDONED	TYPE OF PLACE	LOCATION	REASON	INHABITANTS	CURRENT STATUS
1995	Hospital	Beelitz, near Berlin	Redundancy	Several thousand patients and medical staff	A few buildings restored, most abandoned

IT WAS THE MOST ADVANCED HOSPITAL OF ITS TYPE IN EUROPE, OFFERING MEDICAL CARE AND CONVALESCENCE FOR SUFFERERS OF TUBERCULOSIS. AFTER TREATING TWO BRUTAL DICTATORS AND SERVING AS A WESTERN OUTPOST FOR THE USSR IN THE COLD WAR, IT NOW STANDS AS A PARTICULARLY BEAUTIFUL AND HISTORIC RUIN.

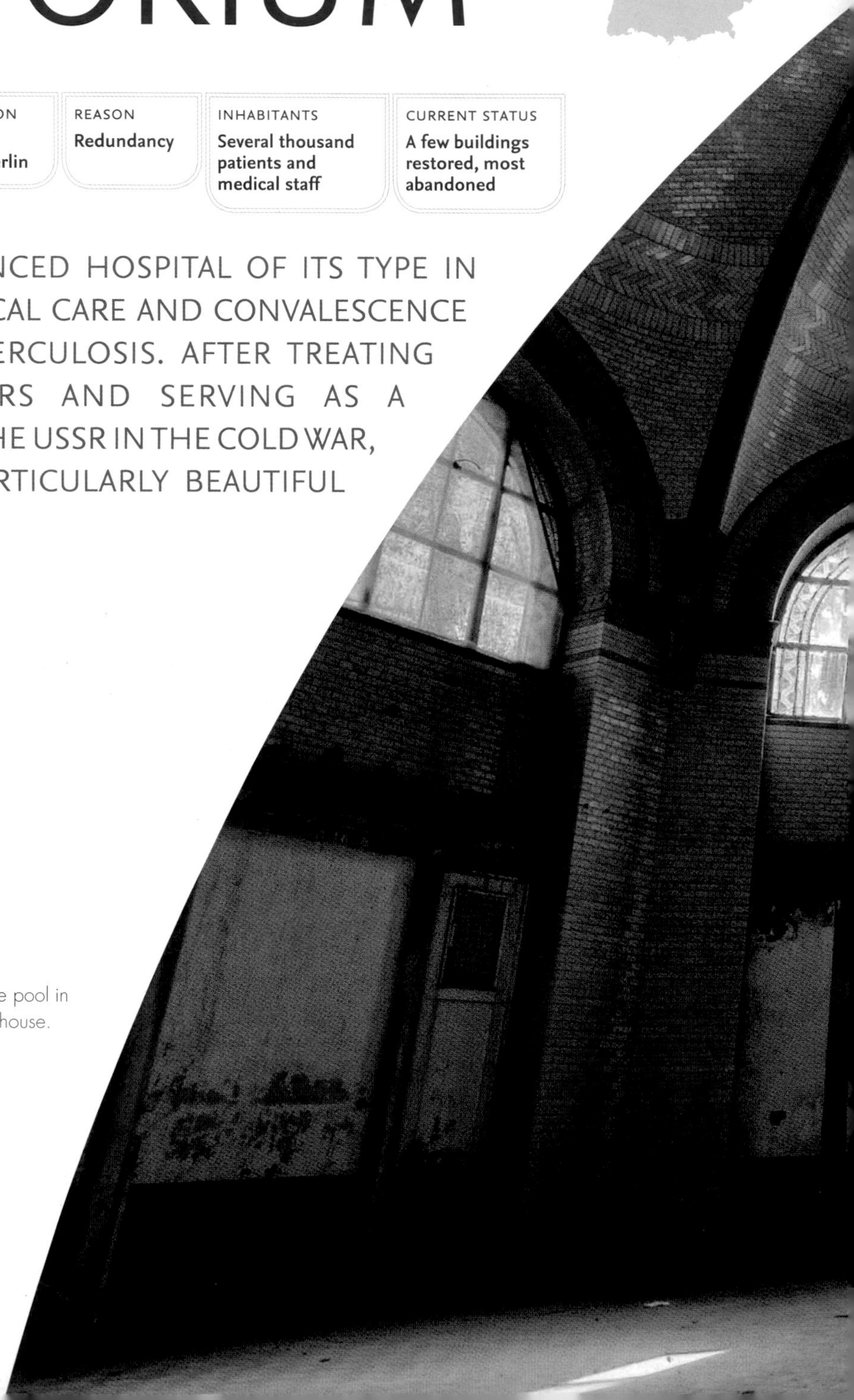

A plunge pool in the bathhouse.

Hitler recovered from his war wounds here during the First World War.

A most beautiful place to die

Beneath the rust and ruin it's clear that Beelitz was one of the most beautiful hospitals in the world. Built in bucolic wooded surroundings isolated from the noise and dirt of everyday life, this sanatorium was so large it functioned almost as a town in its own right. It had sixty buildings, a power generator, railway station, butcher's shop, bakery, post office, stables, restaurants and even its own rifle range.

The magnificent architecture was intended to lift the spirits of the diseased and dying souls who lived here. Tree-lined walkways linked grand pavilions. An ornate dome crowned an exquisitely tiled bathhouse. Humble chimneys were finished in decorative cream and red brickwork.

For nearly a century the hospital led a very eventful life. Then, when the last doctors left in 1995, the surrounding forest moved in. Now every storm knocks some more slates from the roofs, every winter drives the damp even deeper into the beautiful brickwork. It isn't lost yet, though: the hospital was a restricted military site for eighty years and many of its buildings remained untouched during that

time. To walk within their walls is to step back in time to a very different Germany.

Sanatorium supreme

In the late nineteenth and early twentieth centuries Germany was a nation in the throes of empire-building and industrialization. Its expansive ambitions required ever-greater manpower and birth rates soared. However, within the booming cities were dense population pockets where insanitary living conditions gave diseases the chance to flourish. Tuberculosis (TB) was a contagious plague with a virulence that made it the Black Death of its day. Outbreaks swept through European cities in a flash, and at least one in every three people who contracted the disease would die.

German authorities refused to have their workforce scythed down in this way, and they built treatment centres that were the most advanced in the world. The finest of them all was the 'Worker's Consumption Sanatorium', built from 1898–1902 at a site southwest of Berlin. The treatment for TB then primarily consisted of copious amounts of fresh air, lengthy bed rest and a balanced diet to help the body's own defences fight the disease. Aesthetics took precedence over mere function in the design of the buildings, and the country's most respected architects were employed to create a beautiful, peaceful environment that would actively aid patients' recoveries.

Neat clearings were cut in the forest and seven pavilions, or ward blocks, were built. These pavilions had large south-facing verandas that spilled out into rambling grounds. While in Britain TB patients shivered under piles of blankets in wards with the windows thrown wide open, at Beelitz the windows were kept closed and the air was artificially circulated. Pumps and filters cleaned the stale air, which was then warmed before being piped back into the wards.

Once a patient's body began to fight back against the disease, a steadily increasing programme of exercise would be prescribed. Between the buildings were carefully designed gardens with neat paths and resting places where patients could wander at will. The sanatorium and its grounds covered 200 hectares (495 acres) and measured over 1 km (0.6 miles) from north to south. The sanatorium's kitchens, laundries, boiler rooms and other services were sited far from the wards in other parts of the forest to protect the peaceful atmosphere.

In the days before antibiotics, TB was very often treated with surgery and, accordingly, Beelitz had three large operating theatres. The disfiguring and agonizing operations were often as traumatic as the illness itself: several procedures aimed to collapse one of the patient's lungs in order to restrict movement in the chest and so aid healing. This could be done by breaking eight of the patient's ribs; an alternative operation inserted porcelain balls in the chest cavity to crush the lung.

History comes to stay
Beelitz was a very successful facility, with thousands of patients receiving treatment here at any one time, but it only fulfilled its specified function for sixteen years.

When the First World War broke out, the sanatorium was conscripted into use as a military hospital. On 1 July 1916 Britain launched a doomed offensive at the Somme River in France. The horrific battle would result in 195,000 French and 420,000 British casualties; more than 650,000 German soldiers were killed, lost or wounded. Beelitz was flooded with men injured in the battle. In October a 27-year-old corporal who had taken a piece of shrapnel in his thigh at the Somme was sent here to recuperate. He stayed for two months before returning to duty, fully healed and with an Iron Cross (Second Class) on his chest. Unknown at the time, he would later be remembered as the sanatorium's most famous patient – his name was Adolf Hitler.

A Russian hospital in Germany
At the end of the Second World War, Beelitz was used as a military hospital by the Soviet forces then occupying East Germany. It was expanded to become the biggest military hospital outside of Russia, and it continued in this role until 1995.

In 1990, Beelitz admitted its second German dictator: Erich Honecker. The main creator of the Berlin Wall in 1961, Honecker had recently stepped down as leader of Germany – a position he had held since 1971. Honecker stayed in Beelitz for nearly a year, receiving treatment for liver cancer. His walks in the woods were never solitary, though; two Red Army soldiers and a bodyguard stepped behind him all the way.

The *Badehaus*
One of the most exquisite fading gems of Beelitz is the *Badehaus*, or bathhouse. The staircases would not look out of place in an English stately home, with their curved mahogany bannisters and swooping lines. On the first floor are treatment rooms and an airy exercise suite with an arched ceiling supported by colossal wooden beams. Intricately carved dragons decorate each one. Stained glass windows flood the room with coloured light and the view out across the lawns to the nearby buildings is wonderful.

In a cathedral-like circular hall is the plunge pool, set plainly in the middle of the floor. Three enormous multi-paned windows are arranged in a south-facing bay. This room is capped with a large dome and the walls are lined with marble columns. Did the future *Führer* alleviate the pain in his leg with a dip in these cool waters? How often did he look out from those upper windows and gaze into what his future might hold?

Beelitz today
During the Second World War, many buildings were hit by the deluge of Allied bombs dropped on Germany. At Beelitz one of the female pavilions was very badly

damaged, and would never be rebuilt. Today this building has been completely covered with vegetation – trees have even taken root on the roof.

In the surgery buildings at the northwest of the complex, rusting beds still lie in the wards where once patients were prepped for operations. In the theatres themselves the round surgical lightheads still stand, but no bulb has shone within them in decades. Crude graffiti covers many of the walls.

Since the Russian soldiers left for good, the vast hospital's fortunes have been mixed. One medical facility remains: a rehabilitation and research centre for victims of Parkinson's disease. The powerhouse and one of the male pavilions have been restored. The head doctor's villa and the gate lodge houses are private dwellings.

Occasionally the striking buildings and panoramic open spaces have stepped onto the silver screen: *The Pianist* was filmed here in 2002, and *Valkyrie* in 2008. The rest of the hospital's sixty buildings have been locked up and left to their ghosts.

Ultimately, the prognosis for Beelitz is bleak. Since antibiotics were developed in the mid-twentieth century the need for such large sanatoriums has disappeared. Beelitz's sheer size was once its strength – but now is its Achilles' heel. Simply to make the site safe would require extremely expensive remedial work; just for starters, miles of pipes are clad in asbestos bandage. Even after that, finding the patrons, the wealthy health-seekers who would necessarily use and fund the facilities on site ... it seems a stretch to imagine that Beelitz would ever run at full capacity again.

Certainly some of the hospital's buildings deserve to be saved, in recognition of their history and their beauty. Perhaps the outside world will change in time and give Beelitz the chance to reinvent itself once more.

Huge windows brought in light and air to aid recovery.

OBJEKT 825

UKRAINE

Objekt 825

DATE ABANDONED	TYPE OF PLACE	LOCATION	REASON	INHABITANTS	CURRENT STATUS
1996	Secret nuclear submarine base	Crimea	Political	Thousands of military personnel	Abandoned/ Museum

DEEP WITHIN A CRIMEAN MOUNTAIN IS A VAST AQUATIC FACILITY DESIGNED TO HOUSE A FLEET OF SOVIET NUCLEAR SUBMARINES. IN THE COLD WAR, THEY COULD HAVE STRUCK EUROPE WITHIN MINUTES AND IT'S CHILLING TO SEE WHERE DOOMSDAY WOULD HAVE COME FROM.

A curving pen in the Balaklava submarine base.

Battleground of empires

In vast flooded caverns nuclear submarines waited side-by-side in ranked pens. Missiles were wheeled along underground railway lines and then hoisted into place. Storerooms packed to their arched concrete ceilings with gasmasks and radiation suits waited behind thick steel blast doors. Uniformed soldiers scurried down the web of tunnels, obeying urgent orders sent direct from Moscow. Here was a city cut into a mountain, where thousands of people lived and worked in utter secrecy.

If it sounds and looks like a set from a James Bond film, this is no coincidence. This is a very deadly facility constructed at the height of the Cold War, in one of the world's most troubled political powder kegs: the Crimea. This was a top-secret Soviet naval complex from 1961 to 1993 and one of the world's few publically known subterranean submarine bases.

The Crimea is a knuckle of land projecting into the northern waters of the Black Sea. It sits at the crossroads of land and sea routes connecting Europe and Asia: the Balkans are to the west, the Caucasus to the east, Turkey to the south and both Russia and Ukraine to the north. The mightiest of Eurasian empires have been fighting over this piece of land for centuries. In ancient times the Greeks, Persians and Romans all colonized its southern fringe. The Byzantine Empire staked a claim here, as did the Genoese and the Ottoman Empire. These various armies faced off against a prodigious array of war-like, nomadic tribes that advanced from the far-off steppes: the Goths, Cimmerians, Huns, Khazars, Bulgars and the Golden Horde of the Mongol Empire, among many others.

The Russian Empire took control in 1802, and from 1853–1856 it fought off the alliance of Britain, France and the Ottoman Empire in the Crimean War. The Battle of

ABOVE LEFT: The entrance was hidden in a natural harbour used by leisure craft.

ABOVE RIGHT: Mannequins draped in protective cloaks and wearing gas masks.

Balaklava was a major event in this conflict, when the British 'Light Brigade' made their glorious yet doomed cavalry charge against the Russian guns. It was also when the 'Thin Red Line' held out against a Russian cavalry charge. A century later, Balaklava would be the scene of a virtually unknown – but potentially much more deadly – military operation.

After the Second World War the two superpowers, the USSR and the US, embarked on a nuclear arms race that would vastly increase their respective stockpiles of weapons. This Cold War of escalating rhetoric, brinkmanship and threats of pre-emptive strikes created a febrile atmosphere of terror. Leaders on both sides strove to ensure that they had the military muscle to make a decisive pre-emptive strike, or at the very least a cataclysmic retaliatory strike. Preparing for the worst, in the early 1950s Soviet leader Joseph Stalin issued a secret directive – to establish a submarine base from which a formidable retaliatory nuclear strike could be swiftly launched against the West.

Selection as a Soviet base

After a three-year search, Balaklava was chosen as the perfect location. It sits at the end of a fjord-like inlet only 400 m (1,312 feet) across at its widest. This inlet is flanked by high cliffs and has a dog-leg kink that ensures its true length can't be seen from the water. The site offered both shelter from the elements and secrecy from the enemy, and was conveniently close to the major naval base at Sevastopol, home to the Soviet navy's Black Sea Fleet. Perhaps most importantly of all, from here it was a straight run across the Black Sea to the Bosphorus Strait and on to the Mediterranean.

The secret mountain

With the location chosen, the site was given the codename 'Objekt 825' and the nearby city of Balaklava was placed under a heavy blanket of security. An elite team of engineers was drafted in and sworn to secrecy. They were soon working round the clock, drilling into the bay's sheer western cliff. Digging out the 620 m (1,975 feet) long central

canal and 5,000 m² of underground roads, workshops, and arsenals meant removing 120,000 tonnes of rock in the process. The night shift was given a special task: removing the spoil by barge and dumping it at sea in the dark to avoid detection. Construction of the underground complex lasted for four years, from 1957 to 1961.

When they finished they had created an extraordinary high-security warren. The complex's central tunnel could hold seven Class 613 and Class 633 diesel-electric submarines, which were 76 m (250 feet) long and carried cruise missiles. There was space for a further fourteen submarines of varying classes in side galleries. Several could be refuelled at a time, have their batteries recharged and be resupplied with food and fresh water. There were also dry dock facilities, repair shops, and warehouses for storage of torpedoes, missiles and other weapons. The outside of the complex was camouflaged to avoid detection by US satellites. Steel nets were rigged underwater across

the entrance, to keep enemy frogmen from swimming in and sabotaging the site.

With the 600 m (2,000 ft) bulk of Mount Tavros above it and heavy steel doors ready to be shut, the complex could withstand a direct hit from a nuclear bomb with a yield of 100 kilotons (the atomic bomb dropped on Hiroshima had a yield of 15 kilotons). If the bomb should drop, there was room for 10,000 civilians to shelter inside, along with the regular workforce of 300 technicians, engineers and security personnel.

The base was a remarkable feat of engineering, but it had flaws almost from the outset. Three years into construction it was realized that Objekt 825's canals would have to be extended: Russia's new class of nuclear-engined submarines would need an extra 20 m of berth. It had fallen from political favour, too: Nikita Khrushchev was now the Soviet premier, intent on modernizing many of Stalin's military plans. When inspecting the finished complex, Khrushchev reportedly said, 'This should be handed over to the wine makers!'

Post-Cold War cobwebs

His words were prophetic. The complex became increasingly run-down in the last years of the Soviet Union, with vessels that had been sent in for repairs ending up virtually rotting away. The last Russian submarine sailed out of Balaklava Bay in 1995, and the harbour became a virtual scrapheap. The abandoned tunnels attracted looters over the next few years, although at least three such people reportedly died falling down unmarked manholes.

In 2000, the abandoned facility was taken over by the Ukrainian navy, and two years later it was opened as a naval museum. Visitors can see the submarine pens, corridors, workshops, and part of the arsenal where torpedoes, missiles and nuclear warheads were handled. Much of the large underground complex is still off-limits however, behind very securely closed doors.

The future of Objekt 825

Sovereignty of the Crimea is still disputed today. One month after the Ukrainian revolution in February 2014, Russia declared the isthmus part of the Russian Federation; a claim not recognized by Ukraine nor by most of the international community. The future of this region is far from settled. Who knows if armed vessels might once again seek sanctuary within the walls of Objekt 825?

Visitors are shown round the base, which is now a museum.

SATHORN UNIQUE

THAILAND

Sathorn○
Unique

DATE ABANDONED	TYPE OF PLACE	LOCATION	REASON	INHABITANTS	CURRENT STATUS
1997	Residential and retail skyscraper	Bangkok, Thailand	Economic	0	Dilapidated

RISING NEARLY FIFTY FLOORS ABOVE THE SNAKING RIVER AND BUSY STREETS OF THE THAI CAPITAL, THIS WAS TO BE THE LATEST EMBLEM OF THE COUNTRY'S ECONOMIC MIRACLE. NOW IT IS A GHOST TOWER – ITS DREAMS OF THE LUXURY HIGH-LIFE FALLING DOWN AROUND IT.

The ghost in the heart of the city

It was to be a shining sentinel of prosperity: a sleek glass-clad tower that would stand as a proud symbol over one of the world's biggest cities. Today its arching entrance is cluttered with junk and refuse; Romanesque columns are choked by vines, while chunks of masonry fracture and fall to the ground below. The 174 m (570 ft) high would-be wonder is now a cadaver from a more confident era, cut off in its prime.

Thailand's economy was roaring in the early 1990s. It averaged over 9 per cent growth every year from 1985 to 1996 – the highest rate of any country. Easy credit fuelled a construction boom and it seemed that only more good times lay ahead.

In 1990, therefore, the concept of the Sathorn Unique tower seemed a sound one: a 49-storey skyscraper containing 659 luxury apartments and fifty-four retail units exclusively for the biggest and best brand names. The tower would offer a stunning panoramic view of the Chao Phraya River and the city's other glittering symbols of growing wealth. Construction began and progressed smoothly. The building's framework was erected, fitting out was well under way, and by 1996 the building

was 80 per cent complete. Then, almost overnight, it was abandoned.

In May 1997, aggressive speculation in the Thai baht triggered a collapse in the overvalued currency. The Thai stock market fell 75 per cent and the economy ground to a halt. This was the first domino to fall in what would become known as the Asian Financial Crisis.

The workers who had flooded into the capital from rural Thailand and other Asian countries returned home. The Sathorn was just one of many buildings to be abandoned mid-construction.

Symbol of a crash

The Thai economy was back on its feet by 2001, but work never resumed on the Sathorn tower. It remains derelict and crumbling to the point of public danger, right in the heart of the Thai metropolis.

Locals say the skyscraper is haunted: to them it is the 'Ghost Tower'. It is very much off-limits these days, simply for the danger it presents: unguarded sheer drops, glassless windows, rail-less balconies.

Viewing it from outside is an unsettling experience, while the rare photographs that exist of the interior show an extraordinary world reminiscent of a creepy movie set. Wiring spills out of the walls and onto the floor from the walls like the building's very entrails. The floors are a wild mess of abandoned tools, unused building materials, old shoes, rubble, dust and uncapped pipes. In what would have been the foyer, a few marketing brochures promoting the tower in its completed glory lie scattered on the bare concrete floor. Escalators lie gutted, their innards exposed and rusting. Plastic wrappers still trail from their sleek steel exteriors to collect dust. Here is the debris of a decade and a half of ruin.

Up to around floor thirty many of the apartments are tantalizingly close to being completed. They clearly had their floors laid, bathroom suites plumbed in and the fire alarms fitted. Higher than that, the building is a windblown skeleton. Clusters of steel rebar sprout from half-built concrete pillars like decapitated plant stalks. The stairways are as dark as black holes. An opening in the floor is actually an unsealed lift shaft with no lift. One false step up here could mean a forty-floor fall.

The unfinished upper floors are crumbling by the day thanks to humid climate, stormy weather and airborne pollution. Lower down though, in the entrance foyer, the Sathorn Unique has at least picked up a few new tenants: tent-like drapes of fabric, walls of cardboard boxes and scattered cushions are the telltale signs of habitation, the city's less privileged sheltering inside the failed manifestation of its glory.

The irony is that every ruined room and deadly balcony comes with its own million-dollar view of Bangkok; the bustling, life-packed city that is flourishing once again.

MACASSAR BEACH PAVILION

DATE ABANDONED	TYPE OF PLACE	LOCATION	REASON	INHABITANTS	CURRENT STATUS
1990s	Beach resort	Cape Town, South Africa	Environmental	0	Ruined

ONLY SAND WHIPS DOWN THESE WATERSLIDES NOW – THE SWIMMING POOL ITSELF HASN'T SEEN A DROP IN YEARS. WELCOME TO THE BEACH RESORT THAT'S BEING DEVOURED BY THE VERY BEACH IT WAS BUILT ON.

SOUTH AFRICA

Macassar Beach Pavilion

The pavilion in paradise

The view from the top of the waterslide must have been sublime. All around were the rich green grasses of the nature reserve; in front lay the golden strand of the seemingly endless beach. Beyond that rippled the blue waters of False Bay, arcing round in a smooth sweep to the crumpled peaks of the Kogelberg Mountains.

This spectacular location is just half an hour from central Cape Town, and in 1991 some entrepreneurs opened a vibrant beach resort here: the Macassar Beach Pavilion. Fun-loving holidaymakers could explore the brightly painted pavilion with its cafés and kiosks, make a splash in the circular swimming pools, ride waterslides and towel down in the cool blue changing rooms where the sunlight on the wall shimmered like the sea itself.

Nature lovers could explore the Macassar Dunes Reserve, a sandy wilderness of 1,117 hectares (2,760 acres) that nestled behind the pavilion. Signs here warn of 'dunes on the move' and, unfortunately for this resort, they don't lie.

This remote location at the edge of the wild duneland was both the resort's attraction, and its doom. When the sun-worshippers stopped coming at the close of every season, the sand swiftly moved into the ice cream stands and changing rooms. The resort became expensive to clean out every year, and it was abandoned only a few seasons after it had opened.

Season of the sands

Post-abandonment, nature took over in earnest. High tides attacked from the opposite side, burrowing out the sand beneath the resort's foundations. The buildings, slides and pools are now tumbling onto the beach. A few more winters and they will probably be gone completely.

Until then it's the playground of seabirds, butterflies and the occasional kid on a BMX bike. None of them seem to notice that the pavilion's bright summer colours are chipping off into the sand.

PYRAMIDEN

DATE ABANDONED	TYPE OF PLACE	LOCATION	REASON	INHABITANTS	CURRENT STATUS
1998	Coal mining town	Svalbard, Norway	Economic	1,000	Abandoned

JUST 1,000 KM FROM THE NORTH POLE, THIS IS THE WORLD'S MOST NORTHERLY GHOST TOWN. FROZEN IN ICE – AND TIME – IT ILLUSTRATES SOVIET LIFE AND CULTURE AS THEY WERE IN 1998.

Mining coal at the ends of the earth

Snowmobile is the usual means of arrival. Travelling by boat is also possible, so long as the bay is free of pack ice. For almost half the year it's too dark to come here anyway: when the sun dips below the horizon on 4 October it won't show its face again until 9 March. Travel is easier when spring comes: the sun rises on 19 April and will not set again until 23 August.

After a three-hour journey it appears, nestling at the head of a fjord beneath the towering mountain after which it is named: Pyramiden (the 'Pyramid'). Coal mines might not be known for their scenic beauty, but this one has an epic, 'end-of-the-earth' power that captivates all who come here. A vast glacier grinds down from the hinterland. Walrus slide through the raw waters of the bay, looking for seals to snack on.

Visitors stepping out onto the decaying wooden wharf might wonder why their guide always has a bolt-action rifle slung across his back. There's a chance that one might meet the town's new inhabitants – polar bears, which roam through the streets as they will.

There are feral cats, too, which sip from puddles then scurry underneath the pier. Gulls screech and flap at each other over the best windowsills to roost on. That's about as much reclamation as nature is ever going to do here. Trees will never uproot these streets. No ivy will swarm on the buildings. In the icebox of the Arctic, decay is a long-term event.

The mechanics of the coal mine still stand, as if they might be urged back into life at the flick of a switch. The communal buildings and housing of the town are equally well preserved. The roofs are intact, the town square is clear of weeds and rubbish and the ungainly sign carrying the town's name proclaims a welcome. Metal boxes perch on every window ledge of an apartment block; these are fridges. Even in June the temperature never tops 5°C so nature keeps food fresh free of charge.

Lenin stares proudly over Pyramiden's main square – and the mighty Nordenskiold Glacier in the distance. It's the world's most northerly statue of the Soviet leader. In fact, Pyramiden can boast 'the world's most northerly' in many categories: the world's most northerly museum; the world's most northerly swimming pool; the world's most northerly basketball court; and, surreally, the world's most northerly grand piano.

These proud symbols of a thriving modern community seem incongruous now that the town stands in frozen ruin. But they were put there as a showpiece of Soviet civilization, for the West to gaze on and admire.

A sign in the main square marks the town's latitude.

Abandoned instruments in the school music room.

One of the feral cats that now inhabit the old mining buildings.

A Soviet foot in the West

Svalbard is an archipelago that lies roughly halfway between mainland Norway and the North Pole. It is a Norwegian possession but it is also a free economic zone. Whales – and the wealth in their oil – first brought men to these islands. Bases were established in the seventeenth century, to be used sporadically until their eventual abandonment a century later. Coal was the next boom industry, and the mine at Pyramiden was originally sunk by Sweden in 1910. It was sold to Russia in 1927, but remained a very modest operation until after the Second World War. Then a large programme of development began, not only to increase production but also to make a Soviet political statement. The island's status meant that foreigners didn't need a visa to visit, so the Soviets built a showcase society in the Arctic.

Glaciers cover 60 per cent of the archipelago; 30 per cent of the land is barren rock and only 10 per cent holds any vegetation. The patchy soil, where it exists, is feeble and can support only moss. So the Soviets imported ship after ship of soil and grass from Ukraine. In summer the main square shone a verdant green under the permanently blue sky.

Residents used the imported soil to grow fruit and vegetables in greenhouses. They raised chickens, pigs and cattle. The coal provided the town with its own unlimited power supply.

They built a hospital, cafeteria and a 'Palace of Culture' – which featured a library, basketball court, gym and theatre. The architecture was typically Soviet – unadorned yet practical. Many buildings have rounded edges to ease the force of the hard winter wind. In summer, a football pitch was marked out on the thin grass.

The accommodation had a 'student' feel to it, with inhabitants assigned to nicknamed halls of residence. Single men lived in 'London' block, unmarried women in 'Paris' and families in 'Crazy House' – so named for its perpetual hubbub. There were bars, and a heated swimming pool so good that it enticed the children of the town of Longyearbyen to make the cold and boring boat journey over to enjoy it.

By the 1980s the town was home to more than 1,000 people. Russians viewed a contract to work in Pyramiden as a privilege, and the community's upbeat spirit reflected the final glory days of the USSR.

The exodus

In reality, however, the mine at the heart of this apparently thriving community was not profitable. Pyramiden was being subsidised centrally as a piece of living propaganda. When that Soviet image-making machine collapsed in 1991, Pyramiden's days were numbered. Subsidies dried up; there were shortages; salaries and living standards dropped. A tragic plane crash near Longyearbyen in 1996 killed 141 people, including many workers and their families, and caused the already-dipping morale to plummet.

Making the mine profitable would mean accessing larger coal seams deeper inside the mountain. That would mean investment, but in 1997 this was not a priority of the unstable Russian government. In early 1998 the decision was taken to close Pyramiden.

The miners began to depart. Since contracts to work here were usually for two years, the workers didn't bring many belongings with them; and so they simply walked away from the life they had in Pyramiden. That's why today the windowsills still have withering plants, the cafeteria is stacked with clean dishes and sheets lie folded neatly on beds.

All summer long a steady stream of people flowed out by boat and helicopter for Longyearbyen or the still-operating mine at Barentsburg, 100 km (60 miles) to the south, where some of the miners managed to find work.

The last coal was dug out on 31 March, after which the 300 workers who still remained began drifting back to the motherland. The last resident left on 10 October. The winter ice closed in soon after and shut down the town for good.

Pyramiden today and half a millennium hence

This is far too remote a place to tempt looters, and so many wonderful objects remain in situ: musical instruments, sports equipment, costumes in the theatre, and more than a thousand movie reels. Maps, clippings and *Playboy* pinups are still stuck to the walls.

Some experts predict that Pyramiden may still be standing 500 years from today. If the place seems strange and fascinating to us now, how wonderful will this icy time machine seem to our descendants in that far-off day?

LARUNDEL ASYLUM

DATE ABANDONED	TYPE OF PLACE	LOCATION	REASON	INHABITANTS	CURRENT STATUS
1999	Mental asylum	Melbourne, Australia	Obsolescence	750 patients	Derelict

A PIONEERING PSYCHIATRIC INSTITUTION IS NOW THE HAUNT OF GHOST HUNTERS AND DAREDEVIL TEENAGERS. DESPITE THE RUINED WALLS AND EMPTY ROOMS, HERE THE GHOSTS OF THE MOST DAMAGED OF ALL PEOPLE SEEM VERY REAL INDEED.

The main building of Larundel asylum in 2014.

Scared by shadows of the past

Abandoned places can be beautiful, eerie, sad, surprising, epic, historic and wonderful. A few are downright chilling. By the accounts of those who have visited it, Larundel Asylum is in a class of its own when it comes to spookiness.

It was begun in 1938 as part of a huge mental health facility known as Mont Park. During the Second World War it was co-opted for use as a military hospital and training depot. It finally accepted its first psychiatric patients in 1953.

Treating the untreatable

Larundel was where patients suffering from the most acute psychiatric, psychotic and schizophrenic disorders were brought to live their lives. Part of its chilling reputation comes from the fact that this asylum was where the notoriously brutal serial killer Peter Dupas was first treated; and many other severely mentally ill criminals were also treated here. Larundel has also gone down in history as the place where, in 1949, psychiatrist John Cade developed the use of lithium salts to treat mania. Lithium is now in widespread worldwide use as a psychiatric medication.

As pharmaceutical treatments began to replace traditional, institutional care for psychiatric patients in the late 1990s, the Larundel Mental Asylum was one of the many Victorian mental hospitals to be closed down. Some new housing has been built in the asylum's once-extensive grounds and the remaining buildings have been earmarked for future residential development. However, a cluster of dark, dilapidated wards still stands.

An unsettling place to visit

The elements and vandals have taken their toll on the asylum in its years of dereliction. Ruptured ceilings spill their guts to the floors below. The tiles of a bathroom shine with crimson graffiti above a moss-filled tub. A single metal-legged chair stands alone in the middle of a floor covered in shattered glass. Green shrubs surge through broken windows to fill an empty corridor.

Despite – or rather, because of – the gloom and decay, the derelict wards and isolation rooms are a magnet for thrill-seeking youngsters. Some visitors claim to have heard loud banging, children's laughter, sobbing and the

tremulous notes of an old music box. Such tales are hardly surprising: when the sun goes down the broken windows, ruined corridors, echoing wards and history of savage mental illness are like a scary movie scenario made real.

Ghosts in the shell

The asylum is a favoured hunting ground for paranormal investigators, although one doesn't have to believe in the supernatural to feel unsettled here. It is an eerie place on a still, sunny day. In darkness and with a little breeze to rattle the boarded-up windows – not to mention the odd venomous spider, bat or wide-eyed possum making an appearance – well, one's imagination has plenty to work with.

SADDAM'S PALACES

Green Palace, Tikrit ○

IRAQ

DATE ABANDONED	TYPE OF PLACE	LOCATION	REASON	INHABITANTS	CURRENT STATUS
2003	Palaces	Iraq	War	Saddam Hussein and his followers	Military use/ Abandoned

WHEN THE INFAMOUS DICTATOR WAS OVERTHROWN, THE VICTORIOUS ARMY STORMED HIS ABANDONED PALACES AND FOUND ITSELF IN AN EXTRAORDINARY PLAYGROUND OF PINK BOUDOIRS, BALLROOMS, SWIMMING POOLS AND PRIVATE RAILWAY LINES.

BELOW: The train that once brought loyalists to Saddam's VIP resort lies abandoned.

Behind a dictator's closed doors

When a dictator is toppled a whole world of unseen decadence and greed is often abandoned overnight. When Saddam Hussein was ousted in 2003, American soldiers discovered an astonishing collection of luxury residences.

Saddam was in power for twenty-four years and during that time he ordered the construction of around ninety new palaces and mansions. They were built to demonstrate his power and wealth, and to perpetuate his personality cult. Use of the buildings could also be extended to people whom the dictator wanted to reward,

OVERLEAF: Inside the palace of Maqar-el-Tharthar in 2003.

such as high-ranking Ba'ath party officials, friends and family, as well as his numerous mistresses. The palaces were liberally decorated with marble and gold, filled with fine furnishings, swimming pools and luxuries including grand pianos.

After the 1991 Gulf War, Saddam increased the rate of palace building. One of his most notable new structures was the Victory Over America Palace, which commemorated what he saw as a military triumph. The palace was bombed in the second conflict in 2003 however, while still under construction, and was never completed. The boom of a crane damaged by the explosion has slumped onto the building itself. Beside the Victory Over America Palace is the equally preposterous Victory Over Iran Palace.

Pick of the palaces

Saddam celebrated his 62nd birthday in 1999 by building the Green Palace, or 'Maqar-el-Tharthar', close to his home town of Tikrit – 140 km (87 miles) northwest of Baghdad. The palace stands on the shore of the largest lake in Iraq, and is one of the biggest of all Saddam's vanity projects, covering 6.5 km² (2.5 square miles).

The palace had its own railway line running directly to Baghdad and was part of a lakeside resort that included an amusement park. The Green Palace was not a target for Coalition bombs, but it was looted and damaged by Iraqi locals and is now in a ruinous state.

The Republican Palace was Saddam Hussein's favourite place for meeting visiting dignitaries. It was not bombed, as US forces believed that it might hold valuable documents.

Instead it became the hub of American operations inside the secure Green Zone, following the fall of Saddam.

The as-Salam Palace is another huge building, with over 200 rooms, two vast ballrooms, marble flooring and granite walls inlaid with hundreds of thousands of hand-carved and hand-painted flowers. The palace's dome was originally topped with a life-sized statue of Saddam. In the basement is a door that leads down to the network of concrete tunnels that runs beneath Baghdad, joining up other palaces and governmental facilities with Baghdad International Airport. Today that palace is an Iraqi military base.

Who would live in a house like this?

When the Coalition forces took Baghdad in 2003, the American army moved into some of the palaces. Soldiers splashed in Saddam's swimming pools and posed in his former bedrooms, while the huge reception rooms were put to use as offices. The buildings unoccupied by the military were swiftly and comprehensively looted by Iraqi citizens keen to get their hands on some of the trappings of presidential wealth.

Photographers who were on the scene before the looters captured images of a world of luxurious swimming pools, marble columns, huge artworks and tiled floors. Murals and statues of Saddam himself adorned walls throughout the buildings and there were some truly extraordinary sights, such as the bedrooms decorated exclusively in pink satin and velvet.

The palaces have now been handed over to the Iraqi government, and soon they will either be put to an alternative use or demolished.

MIRABEL AIRPORT

CANADA

Mirabel Airport ○

DATE ABANDONED	TYPE OF PLACE	LOCATION	REASON	INHABITANTS	CURRENT STATUS
2004	Airport	Montreal, Canada	Commercial/ Political	0	Awaiting demolition

'THE BIGGEST AIRPORT IN THE WORLD' WAS HOW ITS DESIGNERS ENVISIONED MIRABEL – IT WOULD BE AN OLYMPIC SUCCESS STORY AND A GATEWAY TO NORTH AMERICA THAT WOULD BOOST CANADA'S ECONOMY. BUT IT NEVER TOOK OFF, AND NOW THE UNLOVED TERMINAL IS REDUNDANT.

Montreal takes off

Olympic athletes, journalists and spectators stepped through the splendid, spacious arrivals hall and the whole world watched. It was the summer of 1976 and the terminal at Mirabel was Montreal's brand new gateway to the world.

By the time the Olympics began, Montreal had been booming for a decade. Air passenger traffic was rising by 15–20 per cent a year. The city's airport at Dorval (now officially known as Montréal–Pierre Elliott Trudeau International Airport) was struggling to cope: it had opened in 1941 as an air force station, sending thousands of Allied aircraft on their way to England during the Second World War. It flourished as a commercial airport after the war, and was a major refuelling hub for trans-atlantic flights. In 1960 a new terminal was opened – the largest in Canada and one of the biggest in the world. Montréal–Dorval International Airport became the gateway to Canada for all European air traffic, serving more than two million passengers per year. Government planners predicted that the growth would

continue to the point where Dorval could simply no longer cope: in the early 1970s it was decided that eastern Canada needed a major new airport.

This is an argument that many major cities, such as London, are having now. Is it better to upgrade an old airport that is convenient but cramped, or build a new, bigger and better facility in a more remote location?

Montreal went for option two – and when that failed, switched back to option one. The casualty of that reversal was Mirabel International Airport.

Thinking big

There was certainly no shortage of ambition. The Mirabel masterplan called for six runways and six terminal buildings. A site was selected 39 km (24 miles) northwest of the city and huge amounts of farmland were compulsorily purchased. The airport was to have a large space for industrial development and a buffer zone to limit noise pollution. The

whole site would cover an area of 39,660 hectares (396.6 km²; 98,000 acres). This was larger than the entire city of Montreal, and would have made it the largest airport in the world. This grand plan was never fully realised, however.

When Mirabel opened in 1975, international flights in and out of Montreal were forced to use it in order to encourage the airport's growth. However, domestic flights kept using Dorval Airport. This decision was born out of practical necessity. To get the new airport open in time for the Olympics, it was opened in two stages; the international flights would use it immediately, with domestic departures transferring there a few years later.

The airport's wings are clipped
The result of this was that Canadian passengers wanting to use Mirabel as a hub to fly on overseas faced an inconvenient transfer between airports. Poor travel links made this very inconvenient indeed. Funding for the rapid transit link didn't materialize, and the station that was built in the airport's basement was never connected to the rail network. Moreover, a planned direct highway wasn't built, so passengers had to take a looping route by road from Montreal. Mirabel was simply hard to get to. Travellers and airlines didn't like it, and public pressure made sure that the far more popular Dorval was kept open. Furthermore,

the airport's refuelling business fell away in the late 1970s and 1980s as newer aircraft with a greater range were introduced.

Another factor working against the airport was that the city of Toronto – just 540 km (336 miles) away, not far in Canadian terms – overtook Montreal in growth. Canada's federal government had predicted there would be 17 million passengers at Mirabel by 1985. In reality, it never had more than three million. Toronto, however, was handling 18.5 million by 1991. The area didn't need two airports and it was decided that passenger traffic would be consolidated at an upgraded Dorval. This upgrade happened in the year 2000.

Unclaimed baggage
Mirabel became a cargo airport. The very last commercial flight took off for Paris in October 2004, after which the passenger terminal became instantly redundant.

The cavernous public spaces, intricately designed baggage handling areas and specialist walkways of airports make them hard to adapt to any other purpose. Since it closed, the only major use of the terminal has been as a filming location. Fittingly, the 2004 movie *The Terminal* was shot at Mirabel. At the time of writing the terminal building is scheduled for demolition.

ATHENS OLYMPICS

GREECE
Athens Olympic Venues

DATE ABANDONED	TYPE OF PLACE	LOCATION	REASON	INHABITANTS	CURRENT STATUS
Various	Sporting venues	Greece	Obsolescence	Thousands during the games	Abandoned

HERE THE GREATEST OF ATHLETES BATTLED FOR GOLD AND GLORY. NOW THAT THE OLYMPIC CROWDS ARE GONE THERE IS ONLY DUST AND DEBRIS. MANY OF THESE SYMBOLS OF NATIONAL PRIDE ARE ALSO VICTIMS OF POVERTY AND WAR.

Fleeting dreams of glory

Thousands of workers, millions of hours of effort and billions of pounds flow into the creation of two weeks of supreme sporting spectacle – the Olympic Games. As soon as the notes of the last national anthem fade away, there is little hope for many of the venues themselves. It is the destiny of these epic areas to fade and decay. Even more quickly than the party arrived, its glories are gone forever.

In a way it's understandable that Olympic venues often end up abandoned and falling to pieces. The Games themselves are such a huge, one-off event that the stadiums will never see such use again. To simply maintain them in case of future use would be prohibitively expensive: it will be decades before the event returns to any one country – if ever.

The ideal solution is to repurpose the venues, but this is easier for some sports than others. There may be a community demand for an AstroTurf hockey pitch, but a beach volleyball court may be more difficult to reuse; lots of people go downhill skiing, not so many go ski-jumping. Olympic venues need room for huge numbers of spectators, athletes, TV crews and vehicles to move around – which means they are usually located away from dense population centres. If the dedicated transport links are maintained afterwards, local people can access the venues. But the repurposing costs money, and spending even more after several billions have already been splashed on the event can be politically difficult.

There are usually around seven years of preparation from the time the host city is announced. This intense period of planning and construction builds like a wave that peaks in a glorious two-week run when the whole world is watching. Then, its energy spent in one terrific splash, the waters recede leaving some lonely debris on the beach.

The Games come home

Athens had hoped to host the centenary Olympic Games in 1996, but it lost out to Atlanta. The spiritual home of the Olympics then showed its competitive guts and tried again, winning the honour of hosting the

RIGHT: Ten years after the event, the outfield of the softball stadium runs wild.

OVERLEAF: The stadium that hosted the beach volleyball competitions.

2004 Games. The country took its role as host extremely seriously, spending €9 billion to create a series of stunning sports venues and infrastructure improvements. This was double the original budget, but Athens did get some major assets: a new airport, tram and an upgraded ring road and metro.

The Games themselves were a sporting and cultural success attended by 10,625 athletes from 201 countries competing in 28 different sports, and watched by millions of fans around the world. In the open-air pool Michael Phelps won six gold medals and broke two world records.

Since the Games, their transport infrastructure is still in use and some venues have even gained a new lease of life; the badminton arena is a successful concert hall. However, the table tennis and gymnastics stadiums are eerie shells, on sale but without a buyer in sight. The beach volleyball centre is dusty rather than sandy. The kayak course is a dry concrete bunker. Most venues are permanently locked up to keep out metal thieves. They were scheduled to be converted to community use, but the Greek economic crisis of 2010 stalled this. Now the annual maintenance bill of £680 million is not a priority for a nation being squeezed by austerity measures, and it is likely that most venues will continue to crumble.

SIX FLAGS JAZZLAND

UNITED STATES OF AMERICA

o Six Flags Jazzland

DATE ABANDONED	TYPE OF PLACE	LOCATION	REASON	INHABITANTS	CURRENT STATUS
2005	Amusement park	New Orleans, USA	Natural disaster	Thousands, seasonally	Dilapidated/ Planned rebuilding

WITH ITS TWISTED METAL AND ROTTING WOODEN BUILDINGS, THIS AMUSEMENT PARK STANDS AS A HALF-DROWNED SYMBOL OF THE DEVASTATION THAT HURRICANE KATRINA WREAKED ON THE CITY OF NEW ORLEANS.

Six Flags Jazzland remains submerged on 14 September 2005, two weeks after Hurricane Katrina caused levees to fail in New Orleans.

The deadliest summer

'It's playtime!' ran the theme song of the Six Flags New Orleans amusement park, and to children it was a paradise on earth. Every summer day lines of giddy kids snaked back from the entrance to Mega Zeph, a wild wooden roller coaster; they hung upside down on the Batman ride, made themselves sick on the Zydeco Scream boomerang coaster and happily washed off the mess on the log flume. Very small children flocked to the amusement park with its carousel, SpongeBob SquarePants ride and Pepé Le Pew swings.

This was a place where the local kids turned up an hour before the gates opened, to get in through the turnstiles and onto their favourite rides before the out-of-towners had found their way out of the car park.

The season of 2005 got off to a flying start. The Joker ride had a cool new coat of paint. Word got out that plans were afoot to build a new water park in the resort. Schools in

New Orleans broke up in mid-May and for the next three months the park was buzzing.

Saturday 27 and Sunday 28 August were going to be the last big weekend of the summer. By now most schools in the area had already gone back, but there was still time for one last blowout before the autumn. Mother Nature thought so too.

The perfect storm

Meteorologists first spotted it about 320 km (200 miles) southeast of Nassau in the Bahamas on Tuesday 23 August 2005. It hit the panhandle of Florida as a Category 1 hurricane on the evening of 25 August, with winds of up to 153 km/h (95 mph). This was fierce enough to cause severe damage and kill seven people, but was nothing compared with what was still to come. Hurricane Katrina crossed into the Gulf of Mexico and quickly intensified.

Warm seawater is the petrol in the engine of hurricanes. The water evaporates and condenses in the storm, releasing its latent heat to fuel the tempest further. The Gulf's warm, relatively shallow waters are a bona fide hurricane nursery.

As deadly as a hurricane's wind and pile-driving rain can be, the biggest cause of disaster is usually the storm surge. The hurricane's deep low pressure creates a dome of water in the sea that moves with the storm's eye. The storm's wind pushes the dome up further, to a height influenced by the fetch; that is, the distance across the water that the wind travels over. The longer the fetch and the faster the wind, the more energy the sea has and the higher the surge. The shape of the coastline is an important factor too. Where the shore has a shallow angle, such as at New Orleans, the storm surge is higher than on a steeply shelving coastline. The result is a tsunami-like flood that inundates the land.

Hurricane Katrina reached Category 5 on 28 August, the highest category on the Saffir–Simpson scale, which is used to measure hurricane intensity. A sustained wind of more than 252 km/h (157 mph) will qualify as a 5; Katrina reached 282 km/h (175 mph) with a central pressure of 902 mb when she was 314 km (195 miles) southeast of the Mississippi River mouth.

Katrina veered northwest and then north, setting her sights on Louisiana, where she made landfall at 5.10 a.m. local time on Monday 29 August. The storm had dropped to Category 3 just before hitting the coast, but its winds were still topping 233 km/h (145 mph). Crucially, Katrina maintained a storm surge that is only generally found in Category 5 storms. Although the wind speed dropped, the surge didn't dissipate, maintaining its momentum which it unleashed on the land as it beat a path to New Orleans.

The city as sitting duck
Most of New Orleans is 2 m (6.5 ft) below sea level. It sits in a bowl between the mighty Mississippi River and Lake Pontchartrain, a wide, brackish estuary connected to the Gulf of Mexico. It would seem that this was a foolish place to build a city. But, originally, it was not this low-lying; human activity has caused it to sink relative to the river and ocean.

When founded as a French colonial trading port in 1718, New Orleans' buildings were clustered on the high ground of the river's natural levees. But as the city expanded rapidly in the nineteenth century it spread to the lower areas. In the twentieth century, developers completely ran out of good land, so the city enacted a huge programme of pumping to drain neighbouring swampland for housing. The city also protected itself from flooding with a system of levees, canals and pumping stations.

However, when the Mississippi flooded, as it does naturally and regularly, the 'backswamp' acted as a natural safety valve for the river. Such wetlands actually grow after a flood, thanks to the vast deposit of sediment that the swollen waters bring.

Now the pumping of water made the land subside and it wasn't replenished by new sediment. Dams upriver reduced the amount of sediment carried even more – by up to 67 per cent. Throughout the twentieth century, New Orleans settled so much that it came to lie below the level of the ocean.

Furthermore, the creation of levees and the regular dredging of canals have effectively concentrated the river, 'shooting' its flow further out into the Gulf of Mexico and carrying the remaining sediment far out to sea. The canals have also allowed saltwater to freely ingress landwards, poisoning the freshwater marshes. This has eroded the city's best defences of all: the wetlands and barrier islands off the coast. These have disappeared at an incredible rate – every year of the last half century, 60 km² (23 square miles) of wetlands have disappeared.

New Orleans' low elevation and lack of natural defences combined to make it about as vulnerable as a city could be when faced with a large storm surge.

'The storm that most of us have long feared'
The storm surge was 8 m (25 ft) high when it hit New Orleans. By 9.00 a.m. there was 2 m (6.5 ft) of water in the Lower Ninth Ward, an eastern area of the city near the mouth of the Mississippi River. Two hours later the flood was 3 m (10 ft) deep in St Bernard Parish. At 2.00 p.m. the 17th Street Canal levee was breached. In total the surge punched fifty-three separate holes through the levees in greater New Orleans. Within hours, 80 per cent of the city was submerged.

A cubic metre of water weighs one tonne. This surge was several metres high and kilometres wide, and it broke into a flat city where the buildings were not designed to withstand such a force. It simply swept everything away.

Many areas of the city were obliterated. Now the levees that were designed to protect New Orleans just intensified its pain. The water that had flooded into the city's bowl had no way to get out. It lingered for weeks, increasing death, damage and disease. Corpses floated in the foul, brackish soup of debris, decaying beyond the point of recognition.

Adding up the cost of the damage

Katrina was the costliest natural disaster in US history. Property damage topped $108 billion ($75 billion of which was in the New Orleans area). It was also the deadliest US hurricane since 1928, with 1,833 people killed by the storm and subsequent floods. The failures of the levees in New Orleans are considered the worst civil engineering disaster in US history. Ultimately, more than one million people were displaced from the central Gulf coast, creating the largest diaspora in the history of the United States.

The authorities had expected 800 of the least mobile locals to arrive in the Superdome; in fact, almost 30,000 desperate citizens sought sanctuary there. The emergency services tried to ship in adequate food, water and medicine, but they were overwhelmed. Television pictures of the suffering within the borders of the planet's richest country shocked the world. New Orleans residents, particularly African-Americans whose neighbourhoods suffered the most, were furious at what they saw as neglect by the political class. Their anger still rumbles on today.

Six Flags was a microcosm of what happened to New Orleans. The park was surrounded by a 1.8 m (6 ft) high earthen berm designed to keep floodwaters out. But this was inadequate, and was easily breached by the storm surge. A flood of rain and seawater then filled the park like a lagoon. Drainage pumps designed to remove such an inundation failed, leaving the rides sitting in a 2.1 m (7 ft) deep bath of corrosive salty water for a month. All of the flat rides and 80 per cent of the park buildings were destroyed. Most of the tall rides were badly damaged, and despite Mega Zeph having a steel superstructure specifically designed to withstand hurricane winds, it was condemned. Only Batman was still able to fly.

The park today

In the years immediately following the hurricane, the park rotted as its owners wrangled with their insurance companies. There were several proposals to redevelop the remaining site, but these all fell through and in 2010 the city of New Orleans took ownership of the property.

Since then the park has had an unexpected second life as an atmospheric movie location. The films *Killer Joe, Percy Jackson: Sea of Monsters, Dawn of the Planet of the Apes* and *Jurassic World* have all immortalized its twisted metal and shattered buildings.

TAMPICO

DATE ABANDONED	TYPE OF PLACE	LOCATION	REASON	INHABITANTS	CURRENT STATUS
2007 onwards	City	Mexico	Drug war	297,000	Declining

RIVAL DRUG GANGS ARE SHOOTING UP THE STREETS AND PREYING ON THE CITIZENS. THOSE WHO CAN LEAVE TAMPICO, DO. THIS IS A VERY MODERN ABANDONMENT AND IT IS HAPPENING IN FRONT OF OUR EYES.

BOTTOM LEFT: The city is no longer a draw for young holidaymakers.

Willingly abandoned

Tampico enjoys a warm climate and is blessed with miles of tropical Gulf of Mexico beaches. The town once had a thriving population of 300,000 and was party central for spring-breakers from the US and Mexico. Hordes of young revellers descended on the miles of city beaches and thronged the hundreds of bars to party round the clock. Today nearly all those bars are shut, no one eats in the restaurants and the beaches are just expanses of sand. Parts of a once-joyous city that was known as the 'New Orleans of Mexico' have turned into a Gotham-like nightmare.

Tampico has been hollowed out by fear

The city is the venue for a kill-or-be-killed war between rival drug gangs. There are deadly shoot-outs on crowded streets in broad daylight. Bars are strafed with machine-gun fire.

Arsonists struck at the local oil refinery. A petrol tanker was detonated on a main route into the city. Anyone who is worth anything at all is a potential kidnap target.

There are still plenty of people in the city, but these are the people who have no way of leaving. Those who have been able to get out – the middle classes – have done so, unwilling to risk any more kidnappings. The result is that much of the once-vibrant city centre, and many residential neighbourhoods, have been gutted. Over 200 bars and restaurants have closed in the last few years. Many streets are wild no-go areas where nature or a drug kingpin now rules.

Lush vegetation has commandeered the rooftops. Fast-growing trees punch branches through broken windows and tear up tiled floors. Abandonment on this scale is seldom seen in the centre of a

BOTTOM RIGHT: The exodus has left many majestic buildings, such as the Edificio Maza, to the whims of nature.

major city: where there are so many people around, usually someone will move in to make the deserted place their own. But here it is simply too dangerous. Walk down the wrong street and it could be the last turning you ever take.

Trading chemicals

Tampico was the biggest oil-exporting port in the Americas in the early twentieth century. The oil money financed the construction of many elegant buildings; the town's architecture drew comparisons with Venice and New Orleans. Palm trees cooled the walkways along the rivers and canals. Even after the local oil boom finished, a large refinery here shipped profitable petroleum products to the US. Now hundreds of illicit drug facilities ship even more profitable products north: cocaine, marijuana and methamphetamine.

The strongest cartels, the Zetas and the Cartel del Golfo, control all the usual gang businesses such as drugs, prostitution, pirated goods and extortion. They also run the banks: their men drive the armoured trucks that deliver cash and if they want a property they point a gun to a notary's head and make them sign it away. Almost all the local police force was on the payroll – until the army decommissioned the police. Murdering reporters is another favourite industry: more journalists are killed in this state than in any other in Mexico.

The once-feted historic
centre is a shadow of
its former self.

With no one to stop them, the cartels started by kidnapping the city's wealthiest citizens. There was an exodus of society's top strata as a result. The gangs then went after doctors, lawyers and business owners, and the middle class also fled from the city.

It's hard to imagine this city bouncing back: the violence and crime seems uncontrollable. Perhaps the only hope here is that the cartels themselves follow the money – and relocate to cities with richer pickings. The city might become too poor and rundown to be worth bothering about. That might save Tampico, but it will hardly solve the problem.

NARA DREAMLAND

DATE ABANDONED	TYPE OF PLACE	LOCATION	REASON	INHABITANTS	CURRENT STATUS
2006	Amusement park	Nara, Japan	Economic	Only staff	Abandoned

IT WAS TO BE A JAPANESE DREAM OF DISNEYLAND, BUT WITHOUT THE FAMOUS CHARACTERS, ITS STAR NEVER SHONE AS BRIGHT. ONCE ITS CROWDS WERE LURED AWAY BY MORE GLAMOROUS THEME PARKS ELSEWHERE, THE FLORA AND FAUNA OF THE SURROUNDING WOODLANDS CAME TO PLAY ON THE ROLLER COASTERS, FOOD STANDS AND ARCADES.

Japan dreams of Disney

When Walt Disney opened his fantasy theme park Disneyland in 1955, it wasn't just Americans who flocked to enjoy its brightly coloured Main Street, Sleeping Beauty Castle, rollercoaster rides and larger-than-life characters. A Japanese businessman called Kunizo Matsuo, president of the Matsuo Entertainment Company, visited and was inspired.

The Japanese economy was then bouncing back from the trauma of the Second World War. People had more money, more leisure time and higher aspirations than before. They wanted to have a good time. Matsuo realised that Disneyland offered exactly that.

His concept was to recreate Disneyland in Japan, beside the ancient capital city of Nara rather than Tokyo. This was a somewhat incongruous choice as Nara Prefecture is famed for its ancient monuments, including Buddhist temples, Shinto shrines and the former imperial palace of Heijo, as well as many beautiful parks and forests.

Matsuo worked directly with Walt Disney himself to transfer the Disneyland vision to Japan. The new park would be laid out to a nearly identical plan. There would be copies of the Magic Kingdom's Sleeping Beauty Castle, Main Street USA, Adventureland, the Skyway gondola, the monorail, a pirate ship and several rides including the Tea Party Cup Ride, Submarine Voyage and Flying Saucers. Nara would also have a large wooden roller coaster called Aska, which was based on the Cyclone coaster at Coney Island. It whizzed visitors round rattling curves at 80 km/h (50 mph) and pulled 2.8g when accelerating.

However, just as construction was nearing completion, the licensing deal for the use of Disney characters fell through. The park was named Nara Dreamland, rather than Nara Disneyland and there would be no appearances by Mickey Mouse, Pluto, Donald Duck or Goofy.

Instead the park created its own mascots, Ran-chan and Dori-chan, two children dressed as Grenadier Guards, complete with scarlet tunics and bearskin caps.

The ride is over
Nara Dreamland was popular when it opened, but over the decades it received relatively little investment and its star soon faded. The park's fate was sealed in 1983 when Tokyo Disneyland opened; this was the first Disney theme park to be built outside the United States and it was an instant hit.

Then in 2001, the glamorous Universal Studios Japan resort opened in Osaka, only 40 km (25 miles) away, and Nara's visitor numbers dropped dramatically. By then Nara was already looking tired and past its best. The first Japanese attempt at the Disney dream closed its doors on 31 August 2006.

No holiday-makers come here now. The only regular visitors are humourless security guards patrolling for vandals. The few photographers who have made it in have sent back eerie images of a fantastical playland being slowly engulfed by nature.

Land of lost theme parks
There are many abandoned amusement parks around the world, and Japan seems to have a high proportion of them. Nara had a sister park – Yokohama Dreamland – which opened in 1964 and had a similar design and rides. It closed even sooner, in 2002, and was razed to the ground. A prison was built on the site.

In Yamanashi Prefecture, Gulliver's Kingdom offered spectacular views of Mount Fuji but little in the way of excitement for visitors. The colossal supine figure of Gulliver was the main attraction, but the park's rides were limited to a bobsled track and a luge. It was largely built with government money supplied to stimulate the economy, and was something of a white elephant. Admissions were low throughout its ten-year lifespan and it closed for good in 2001. The 45 m (147.5 ft) long Gulliver was demolished in 2007 along with his Kingdom.

KANGBASHI NEW AREA

DATE ABANDONED	TYPE OF PLACE	LOCATION	REASON	INHABITANTS	CURRENT STATUS
c. 2009	New-build city	Inner Mongolia, China	Economic	c. 20,000 out of 1 million	Under construction

IT WAS TO BE A CHINESE DUBAI: A BRAND NEW CITY WITH GOVERNMENT OFFICES, THRIVING BUSINESSES, SCHOOLS, THEATRES AND A MILLION INHABITANTS DEEP IN THE ARID MONGOLIAN DESERT. BUT NEARLY TEN YEARS AFTER THE FIRST STRUCTURES ROSE FROM THE SANDS, 98 PER CENT OF KANGBASHI STANDS EMPTY. WELCOME TO THE LARGEST GHOST CITY IN THE WORLD.

Life in the emptiest town on earth

Rows of unfinished concrete tower blocks march to the desert horizon. Road junctions – built extra wide to cope with traffic – are dusty and carless. Whole neighbourhoods of identical villas wait for their first resident.

A pair of colossal horses rear in the middle of a vast central plaza. A sunburst of grassed strips is supposed to radiate around them to further glorify this epic public space. However, the plaza is brown and blown with dusty sand. This is a city where one can drive for kilometres, past block after block, and never see a soul.

Two things make Kangbashi extraordinary. First is its sheer size – this is a city the size of San Diego or Glasgow. Secondly, most of it was never occupied in the first place. To understand how such a huge city could grow from bare sand and yet remain so empty, it's necessary to examine the explosive success of the Chinese economy in the late twentieth century.

China's economic miracle

The adage that Rome cannot be built in a day is true – it's actually two months. Throughout the decade 2002–2012, that's how long it took China to construct the equivalent of a major European city. After the death of communist leader Mao Zedong in 1976, the most populous nation on the planet awoke from decades of economic hibernation and raced to catch up with the world's major powers.

In the early 1980s new leader Deng Xiaoping had enacted a bold programme of reform. Private enterprises were encouraged, and the country's economy began to blossom. Over the next thirty years, China would post annual GDP growth rates of 9–10 per cent per annum. In 2011 China overtook Japan to become the world's second-largest economy; and the Chinese region with the nation's highest gross domestic product per capita was Inner Mongolia.

TOP RIGHT: The horses symbolize the strength of Genghis Khan's Mongolian hordes.

BOTTOM RIGHT: The statues' silk scarves are washed and replaced weekly.

OVERLEAF: Field of dreams: it's built, but no one has come.

The land of black gold

Inner Mongolia is an autonomous region of China that was established in 1947. Much of Inner Mongolia is desert or steppe. Savage sandstorms are a daily fact of life, and the region has very long, cold winters with frequent blizzards. But underground, this is a rich and fruitful land: Inner Mongolia has huge reserves of iron ore, rare earth minerals and one quarter of the world's coal reserves.

With China's economic dragon in full flight, Inner Mongolia was perfectly placed to profit, and the glowing heart of the area's economic fire was Ordos City. This is less a metropolis than a vast administrative area covering 86,752 km² (33,495 square miles) of the Ordos Desert. Its urban nucleus is Dongsheng, which had a population of 582,544 in 2010.

Coal output here doubled from 260 million tonnes a year in 2005, to 500 million tonnes in 2010. A generation before,

most people in this desert plain had watched the sun set through the open flap of their tent. Now many viewed it through the tinted windscreen of a Land Rover. It was here in 2004 that the idea for Kangbashi was born.

New area, new era

Local government officials in Dongsheng looked at the coal taxes filling up their coffers and ordered a vast new city district to be built from scratch in an empty area 24 km (15 miles) to the south: Kangbashi New Area.

This location was blessed with one of the few reservoirs in the region. The streets were to have exotic international names, such as Exquisite Silk Village, Kanghe Elysees and Imperial Academic Gardens. With a property boom sweeping across China, buyers were intoxicated. Properties in Kangbashi were snapped up. They couldn't be built fast enough.

But the properties were being bought by investors from distant cities rather than migrating workers. As the prices continued to rise, their investments looked increasingly sound and more investors joined in, driving demand – and prices – ever higher. Virtually all the properties were empty, but the market was buoyant. It was beginning to look like a bubble.

The mood changed in 2009. House prices had risen so high that new investors were put off, and even fully completed apartments became difficult to sell. As real estate sales weren't made, loans went unpaid and investors pulled out before projects could be completed – leaving entire streets of unfinished buildings. Just as quickly as money had poured into Kangbashi it poured out again. Developers began to slash prices. In 2014 the average house cost $470 per square foot, down from $1,100 in 2009. The investors stopped investing and Kangbashi went into hibernation.

The city with everything but people

For Kangbashi's few inhabitants life must be pleasant, if rather odd. There are offices, government buildings, museums, theatres and sports fields, all surrounded by acres of suburbs overflowing with middle-class duplexes and bungalows. Best of all, there is no rush hour.

The residents are optimistic, still fully believing the venture will be a success. This means that unlike many abandoned places Kangbashi is still cared for. Every day a veritable army of caretakers and cleaners works to keep the city spick and span and ready for business. Often they are the only people on the streets. In an immaculate football stadium a man cleans the seats, mows the grass and paints the lines. Yet no games have been played here. Nearby, some bronze sculptures of children have real silk scarves knotted round their necks. These scarves are removed, washed and neatly retied every week.

An empire reborn

Much of the city's public sculpture celebrates the epic empire-building of the Mongol warrior, Genghis Khan. Eight centuries ago his hordes on horseback swept across much of Asia, creating the largest contiguous empire the world has ever seen. To the planners of Kangbashi this history of fierce, romantic independence echoes the boldness of their own vision. Ironically, though, the great Khan didn't have much to do with this specific area at all – he was born far to the north and his rule was concentrated there and to the west.

The Mongol determination is evident in the fact that construction is still going on. In the day, workmen add the finishing touches to the pavements of a plaza surrounded by empty offices. Drive round at night and one might see a swarm of welders' arc-lights glowing like fireflies in a half-finished tower.

Will they ever complete this gargantuan building project in the desert? It seems unlikely. But thirty years ago no one could have conceived of such a place existing at all. Just as the very concept of Dubai would have seemed ridiculous five decades ago, it may be that one day the visionaries who were bold enough to dream of Kangbashi will see their ambition fully realized, and the city will flood with life.

INDEX

Page numbers in **bold** refer to information contained in captions.

Photography Credits

Editorial Credits
Text by Richard Happer
Layout and maps by Mark Steward
Edited by Karen Midgley
Index by Lisa Footitt
Editorial Consultant: Darmon Richter – www.thebohemianblog.com